DANGEROUS KIDS

Also from the Boys Town Press

Books for Parents or Professionals

Teaching Social Skills to Youth
Treating Youth with DSM-IV Disorders: The Role of Social Skill Instruction
Building Skills in High-Risk Families: Strategies for the Home-Based Practitioner
Skills for Families, Skills for Life
Common Sense Parenting® (also in audio)
Angry Kids, Frustrated Parents
Rebuilding Children's Lives: A Blueprint for Treatment Foster Parents
Effective Skills for Child-Care Workers
Caring for Youth in Shelters
Working with Aggressive Youth
Unmasking Sexual Con Games: Helping Teens Identify Good and Bad Relationships
The Well-Managed Classroom
La Crianza Práctica de los Hijos (also in audio)

Books for Teens

A Good Friend: How to Make One, How to Be One
Who's in the Mirror? Finding the Real Me
What's Right for Me? Making Good Choices in Relationships

Videos

Common Sense Parenting® Learn-at-Home Video Kit
Helping Your Child Succeed
Teaching Responsible Behavior
Boys Town Videos for Parents Series

For a free Boys Town Press catalog, call 1-800-282-6657.

The Boys Town National Hotline, 1-800-448-3000, is a 24-hour crisis hotline for parents and children struggling with any problem.

DANGEROUS KIDS

**Boys Town's Approach for Helping Caregivers
Treat Aggressive and Violent Youth**

Michael Sterba, M.H.D.
Jerry Davis, Ph.D.

BOYS
TOWN
PRESS

Boys Town, Nebraska

Dangerous Kids

Published by the Boys Town Press
Father Flanagan's Boys' Home
Boys Town, Nebraska 68010

Publisher's Cataloging-in-Publication

(Provided by Quality Books, Inc.)

Sterba, Michael.
    Dangerous kids : Boys Town's approach for
helping caregivers treat aggressive and violent
youth / Michael Sterba, Jerry Davis. -- 1st ed.
    p. cm.
    Includes index.
    ISBN: 1-889322-31-8

    1. Behavior therapy for teenagers. 2. Behavior
therapy for children. 3. Aggressiveness
(Psychology) in adolescence. 4. Aggressiveness
(Psychology) in children. 5. Child
psychopathology. I. Davis, Jerry, 1947- II.
Father Flanagan's Boys' Home. III. Title.

    RJ506.V56S84 1999   616.89'142
                      QBI99-397

10   9   8   7   6   5   4   3   2   1

Acknowledgments

This book would not have been possible without the dedicated and ongoing efforts of many people. We would like to thank the following Boys Town administrators and staff for their contributions to this book: Father Val J. Peter, Executive Director; Jack Nelson, Senior Training Specialist; Ron Herron, Director of the Writing Division; and Dr. Robert Larzelere, Director of Residential Research.

A special thanks to Dr. Patrick Friman, Director of Specialized Clinical Services and Research at Boys Town, for allowing us to use selected portions of his research study in this book. Dr. Friman's help and cooperation is greatly appreciated.

Table of Contents

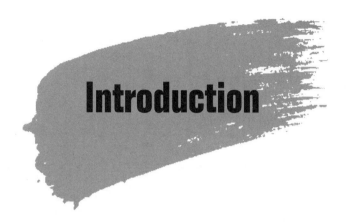

Introduction

Littleton, Colorado – Two heavily armed young men wearing black trench coats attack Columbine High School, firing shotguns and setting off bombs. When the carnage ends hours later, 12 students and a teacher are dead, and 23 others are wounded. The two attackers – both seniors at Columbine – kill themselves with their own guns in the school library.

Jacksonville, Florida – A 14-year-old boy is arrested after the decomposing body of an 8-year-old neighbor girl is found hidden in his bedroom. She had been stabbed and beaten to death. The young boy confesses and is charged with murder.

Columbia, South Carolina – Two brothers, ages 11 and 13, are charged in the beating death of their 6-year-old cousin. Police say the boys and their mother beat the girl for getting off at the wrong school bus stop.

Clearfield, Pennsylvania – A 14-year-old girl is sentenced to six months in a juvenile detention center for tightening a noose around the neck of a shy girl with a learning disability, then watching as friends bludgeoned the girl with a rock, killing her. Three other teenagers are charged with homicide.

Springfield, Oregon - One day after being arrested and suspended from class for bringing a gun to Thurston High School, a 15-year-old boy opens fire with a semiautomatic rifle on a crowd of students in the school cafeteria. Two students are killed and 22 others are wounded. The boy had shot his parents to death earlier.

Onalaska, Washington – A 15-year-old boy points a 9 mm semiautomatic pistol at his girlfriend and threatens to kill her if she doesn't get off the school bus with him. He then takes her to his home and fatally shoots himself as the girl's father tries to break down the door.

Fayetteville, Tennessee – Just three days before his graduation, an 18-year-old honor student opens fire in a parking lot at Lincoln County High School. He kills a classmate who was dating his ex-girlfriend.

Pomona, California – While playing basketball at a local elementary school, two teenage boys are shot and killed by a 14-year-old boy only hours after classes end. A third boy is wounded. The shooting is blamed on a rivalry between two groups of youths.

Edinboro, Pennsylvania – A 14-year-old student at James W. Parker Middle School fatally shoots a 48-year-old science teacher in front of classmates during a graduation dance.

Daly City, California – At Fernando Rivera Middle School, a 14-year-old boy shoots at his principal in a crowded courtyard at the beginning of the school day. The shot misses and no one is hurt. The boy then tosses the small handgun in a bush and returns to school for math class. The youngster was angry over being sent home by the principal the previous school day after an incident that involved a friend of the boy.

Jonesboro, Arkansas – Four girls and a teacher are shot to death in a schoolyard during a fake fire drill at Westside Middle School; ten others are wounded. Students and teachers were lured outside when an 11-year-old boy set off a fire alarm. The boy then joined another boy, age 13, in the nearby woods, and the pair opened fire with rifles on the defenseless and unwitting victims once the fire exit doors locked behind them.

West Paducah, Kentucky – A 14-year-old student shoots and kills three classmates and wounds five others while they take part in a prayer circle at Heath High School. One of the wounded girls is paralyzed.

Pearl, Mississippi – A 16-year-old boy kills his mother, then goes to Pearl High School and shoots nine classmates. Two students are killed, including the boy's ex-girlfriend.

What's Happening to Our Kids?

Why are today's youngsters turning to such deadly and violent acts to solve their problems? Society is struggling to answer this tough question. It seems incomprehensible that kids could be killing and assaulting kids and adults, but it's occurring at an alarming rate. Understanding and dealing with aggression and violence in children and adolescents is a difficult and complex issue. Yet, it is a problem that must be addressed and corrected if youngsters are to learn to peacefully coexist with others in society and ultimately lead happy and successful lives.

Many current trends are being blamed for this frightening phenomenon. Some people cite the soaring divorce rate and single-parent homes; others say youth have become desensitized to violence by what they see in the movies, on television, and in video games. The glamorization of brutal conduct that dominates music lyrics and videos also is seen as a culprit. Still others argue that the availability of weapons like knives and guns (one-third of all households have at least one gun), or the use and abuse of drugs and alcohol have led to these shocking incidents of aggressive and violent acts by children and adolescents.

Separately, none of these factors is probably the root cause of aggression and violence. However, it is possible that a compilation of these factors strongly influences youth who already have a propensity to use aggression and violence as a way of coping with life's obstacles. A youth's aggressive and violent tendencies can be fueled and validated by all these influences. In other words, these kids may be getting the message that it's okay to lash out in destructive and hurtful ways.

Biology (neurotransmitters and genetics) and psychosocial processes (thoughts and feelings) often have a direct impact on a youngster's aggression and violence problem, and they can play a crucial role in a child's treatment. However, Boys Town also believes that most youth who choose aggression and violence have learned or been taught, often unwittingly, to use these kinds of abusive behaviors by others in their environment (e.g., parents, other adults, caregivers, siblings, friends, etc.). They learn that aggression and violence are options for solving problems from seeing others who are influential in their lives frequently use these behaviors. Most of these same aggressive and violent youngsters haven't had the opportunity to learn more positive ways of coping with and solving disagreements they have with others. Simply put, these kids just don't know any other way to handle difficult, frustrating, or upsetting situations that inevitably arise.

Boys Town knows these kids well. Our professionally trained staff have worked with and helped thousands of aggressive and violent youth in a variety of settings. As a result, Boys Town has designed and developed some excellent strategies that can reduce aggression. These strategies are at the heart of the Boys Town Teaching Model, a model that teaches children and adolescents self-control and is extremely effective with aggressive and violent youngsters.

Many youth have long histories of using aggressive and violent behavior. Aggressive kids have learned that being a bully and intimidating others or violently lashing out when things aren't going their way is an effective way of getting what they want. Over time, these behaviors become deeply ingrained in the way these youth interact with others.

Boys Town believes that one very important component in helping children and adolescents overcome their aggression problems is teaching prosocial skills and behaviors that can take the place of the aggressive and violent behaviors that have been used in the past. In addition, these same youngsters may have a certain biological condition that requires medication, or have faulty psychosocial processes that need to be corrected. Possibly expanding treatment to include all three areas not only can reduce aggression and violence, but also allow youngsters to get their needs met in a more socially acceptable manner.

Boys Town knows kids can change. We've seen it happen time and again with youngsters whom others have given up on. Throughout Boys Town's long history, many youth – including aggressive and violent kids – have learned to cope with and respond to anger, frustration, disappointment, and other unpleasant feelings in new, appropriate ways that enable them to lead happy, productive lives.

The goal of this book is to better equip caregivers with interventions, treatment options, and Treatment Plans for teaching aggressive youth how to replace unhealthy, antisocial, and destructive ways of behaving with ways that are healthy, socially acceptable, and safe. It provides a clear picture of aggression, and offers some practical, effective short- and long-term ideas and strategies for defusing aggression in youth. This approach can be used by any adult – teachers, school counselors, social workers, probation officers, psychologists, foster parents, child-care staff and administrators, and other professionals – who is responsible for shaping children's lives.

What Is in This Book?

There are four parts to this book. In the first part, Chapters 1 and 2 define what aggression is (and what it is not) and introduce and discuss two different types of aggression and how to identify each one. In addition, there is an exploration of some of the most respected and current theories about why kids become aggressive, along with the importance of understanding these reasons. Some of Boys Town's own studies will be introduced to provide insight into aggression in youth.

The second part of this book includes Chapters 3, 4, 5, 6, and 7. These chapters contain a description and explanation of how to deal with aggressive behavior through the proven teaching methods developed at Boys Town and incorporated into the Boys Town Teaching Model. There will be an explanation of each teaching method and how it helps to bring about change in a child's behavior. These methods meet a wide range of needs, from teaching skills before they will be used to correcting negative behavior to praising positive behavior. Also presented is research data that show that kids – including aggressive kids – who receive treatment that is based on the Boys Town Teaching Model get better.

Chapters 8, 9, and 10 form the third part of this book. Here, there is a discussion of treatment planning and the various treatment strategies that can be utilized to help children and adolescents reduce aggressive behaviors. Sample treatment plans from a variety of settings will be presented to help caregivers see how intervention strategies can be developed for aggressive youth and used in different environments.

In the fourth part of this book, Chapter 11 examines the importance of creating and maintaining a safe treatment environment for kids and caregivers. In addition, the various rights that youth in treatment have will be discussed.

Finally, an appendix at the end of the book offers a social skills chart that can be used as an easy reference guide for caregivers as they teach new, prosocial skills to replace old, aggressive behaviors. This chart not only lists skills, but also shows which skills work best with specific types of aggressive behaviors.

We hope you find this book useful in your work with children and adolescents. Aggression and violence in youngsters is an extremely troubling and complex issue in today's society, especially for those caring adults who take on this problem every day. Helping a child overcome his or her aggressive behaviors requires patience, vigilance, knowledge, and experience. Our desire is to provide some sound and useful strategies for developing clear and effective treatment interventions that can help you lead troubled youth back to the path of success.

"Our young people are our greatest wealth. Give them a chance and they will make a good account of themselves."

Father Edward J. Flanagan
Founder of Boys Town

CHAPTER 1

Aggression:
What It Is and What It Is Not

Aggression, like a chameleon, often takes on a different appearance to different people. A child's behavior that one person considers harmless may be seen as a sign of serious problems by someone else. That is why it is imperative that caregivers adopt a standard definition for aggression as they learn new ways of dealing with children and youth who display aggressive behaviors. An accurate definition and a solid understanding of what aggression is (and what it is not) are absolutely necessary before effective treatment plans can be developed.

According to Lange and Jakubowski (1976), aggression is defined as "...directly standing up for one's personal rights and expressing thoughts, feelings, and beliefs in a way that is often dishonest, usually inappropriate, and always violates the rights of the other person." This definition also applies to a situation where a person behaves in an aggressive manner on behalf of another person (e.g., two youngsters are arguing; a friend of one of the youngsters suddenly steps in and punches the other person). The definition is a good one because it goes to the heart of the most negative aspect of aggressive behavior – hurting others.

Obviously, many behaviors can fall within this definition: arguing, fighting, taking something from someone, calling others names, pushing and shoving, hitting, kicking, showing disrespect, and making fun of others. And all kids engage in these and other negative behaviors as part of normal development. Aggression becomes a serious problem, however, when a pattern of such behaviors develops and a youngster routinely uses aggressive behaviors to get his or her needs met, or when the intensity or severity of these behaviors increases. Then caregivers must act quickly to prevent these behaviors from getting worse or becoming ingrained in a youth's personality.

Aggression is a complex and difficult problem. There are no easy answers that can make aggressive and violent behavior magically disappear from a youngster's life. Helping youngsters overcome their aggression problem requires hard work, tenacity, and creativity from caregivers.

The earlier adults recognize that children are turning to aggression and intervene, the more likely it is that these youth can learn positive ways to interact with others and get what they want. The hope for aggressive children lies in the ability of caregivers to recognize and acknowledge that youth are developing aggressive habits, and to take action in a positive, effective manner. Steering kids away from aggression and back to a path that can lead them to success at home, in school, on the job, and in life, is the only option.

Aggression doesn't occur in a vacuum; many factors can affect how a child behaves in different situations (e.g., the child's relationship with a person he or she is interacting with, how badly a child wants something, a problem at home or school that a caregiver is unaware of, how a youngster slept the previous night, and so on). Some days there are no signs of aggressive behavior and you see only a charming, loving child. Many days, you might deal with less-severe forms of aggression. Other days – more than you care to experience – aggressive and even violent behaviors will dominate the child's personality. Understanding and effectively dealing with the day-to-day occurrences of less-severe aggressive behaviors like noncompliance, teasing, whining, and scolding before they escalate to hitting, kicking, vandalism, and in extreme cases, serious physical assault, is one of the important ways of helping children learn self-control skills and other positive alternative behaviors.

In recent years, it seems that the most severe forms of aggressive behaviors – assault, rape, murder – are occurring with greater frequency. However, not all aggressive kids commit these types of vicious and extreme acts of violence. Aggression comes in many different shapes and sizes. The majority of aggressive youth engage in more subtle forms of aggressive behavior. For example, a daughter might whine and complain every time her parents ask her to clean up her messy room in order to get out of doing the task. Or a male student might glare at a teacher while she is criticizing his poorly done assignment, hoping to intimidate her so she won't have him redo it.

These types of lower level aggressive behaviors are harder to detect and many times are overlooked and ignored. The danger here is that, left unattended, these behaviors are reinforced and can actually escalate over time. Recognizing and treating aggression at its lowest levels can prevent kids from resorting to more severe forms of aggression, including violence.

This chapter will discuss the five levels of severity in aggression – from subtle behaviors to overt, violent acts – and provide some examples of behaviors at each level.

There also will be a detailed explanation of proactive and reactive aggression. Understanding and identifying the behaviors that make up these two distinctly different types of aggression enables caregivers to develop appropriate intervention strategies. Included in this chapter will be a discussion of bullying, a common and frustrating problem for kids of all ages.

Anger and assertiveness are often mistaken for aggression. To give parents and caregivers a clearer picture of aggression, a short discussion, along with examples, is included to help clarify this misconception. Key issues in the development of aggression and violence in youth will be explored so that caregivers can have a richer, comprehensive picture of aggression.

To begin, let's take a look at how the problem of aggression among young people has grown.

Scope of the Problem

Unfortunately, aggressive and violent behavior is all too common among today's youngsters, and in fact, is on the rise. The U.S. Department of Justice's Office of Juvenile Justice and Delinquency Prevention (OJJDP) states in its report, *Juvenile Offenders and Victims: 1997 Update on Violence* (Sickmund, Snyder, & Poe-Yamagata, 1997), that "a greater proportion of violent crimes were attributed to juveniles in 1994 and 1995 than in any of the last 20 years."

Historically, the Violent Crime Index compiled by the Federal Bureau of Investigation (FBI) has been the nation's barometer for violent crime. The Index collects information on the crimes of murder and nonnegligent manslaughter, forcible rape, robbery, and aggravated assault. The FBI document, *Crime in the United States 1995*, reported that between 1986 and 1995, there was an astonishing 67 percent increase in juvenile arrests for these four crimes. This alarming trend indicates that more and more youth are turning to aggression and violence as a way to solve problems and disputes, and that they are committing violent acts like murder, rape, robbery, and assault more often than their counterparts 10, 15, or 20 years ago.

Research on youth aggression and violence reveals other disturbing findings. Butts, Snyder, Finnegan, Aughenbaugh, and Poole (1996) report that "between 1985 and 1994, delinquency case rates increased 30 percent or more for every age group between 13 and 17." Furthermore, between 1985 and 1995, violent crime arrest rates increased 70 percent for persons between the ages of 15 and 18 (Sickmund, Snyder, & Poe-Yamagata, 1997). Finally, Patterson, Forgatch, Yoerger, and Stoolmiller (1998) found that youth who engage in antisocial acts – including aggression – as early as age 9 or 10, are arrested for the first time by age 14, and have three or more arrests before age 18 are likely to become chronic and violent juvenile offenders. The bottom line is that today's youngsters not only are more likely to be involved in acts of delinquency that include aggressive and violent behavior, but also are beginning to commit these acts at earlier ages. These acts also are increasing across all age groups.

Turning to anger, aggression, and violence as a way of coping with life's challenges can deal a devastating blow to a child's efforts to become a productive and valued member of society. Children who learn and adopt these behaviors have trouble making and keeping friends, and their relationships with parents and siblings can be damaged or destroyed.

Adults label them as "troublemakers" or "dangerous" or "delinquents," and eventually, well-intentioned people (teachers, coaches, counselors, youth group leaders, etc.) who want to help, stop trying as frustration and despair set in. Instead, they turn their attention to the kids who want to learn and grow. Ultimately, children who choose aggression and violence fail in school, on the playground, in the neighborhood, and at home.

Left unchecked, these harmful behaviors become more polished and carry over into adulthood where they can result in more insidious aggressive acts. Spousal and child abuse, drug and alcohol abuse and dependency, robbery, and assaultive criminal activity become the norm, destroying the prospects of having a good job, a happy marriage, and a loving family.

Five Levels of Severity in Aggression

Aggression can develop along a continuum and vary in degrees. The behaviors along this continuum are diverse and become drastically more harsh as youth move from lower-level behaviors like noncompliance and yelling to higher levels like assault and murder. However, the common factor that binds all these aggressive behaviors together is the end result: Kids get their way or get their needs met.

Knowledge of the wide variety of behaviors that make up aggression enables parents and caregivers to assess the seriousness of a child's problem. This is the first – and perhaps the most important – step in developing appropriate and effective treatment strategies for troubled youngsters.

Through extensive research and many years of experience working with thousands of aggressive and violent children and adolescents, Boys Town has identified five levels of aggression. (See Figure 1.)

Figure 1

Five Levels of Severity in Aggression

Level I – Noncompliance and/or Making Threatening Statements or Gestures

A youngster regularly responds with subtle forms of aggression and/or verbal and nonverbal threats.

Examples (Noncompliance):

Youth repeatedly refuses to do what a parent, teacher, or other authority figure asks

Whining and crying

Sarcastic responses – youth responds with a voice tone that conveys the message, "Don't bug me"

Criticism – youth responds with verbal or nonverbal negative criticism of another person's behavior or characteristics

Teasing

Examples (Threats):

Using demanding statements (e.g., "Make me something to eat!")

Repetitive verbal or nonverbal behavior that is intended to annoy (e.g., repeatedly pounding a fist on a table)

Staring and glaring

Clenching a fist or both fists

Cursing and yelling

Ultimatums (e.g., "If I can't go to the movie, I'm gonna kick your a--!")

Invading someone's personal space

Physically aggressive posturing (e.g., towering over a person in a threatening manner)

Verbally threatening another person or self

Level II – Causing Property Damage

A youngster frequently responds with actions that damage property.

Examples:

Throwing objects

Punching or kicking stationary objects (e.g., punching or kicking a hole through a wall)

Vandalism

Stealing

Fire-setting

Arson

Level III – Harming or Killing Animals

A youngster frequently is cruel to animals, or tortures or kills them.

Examples:

Hitting or kicking an animal

Poisoning an animal

Stabbing or shooting an animal

Torturing an animal

Setting an animal on fire

Level IV – Physically Harming Others or Self

A youngster consistently responds with a behavior that physically hurts others or self, but does not produce long-lasting or permanent physical or psychological damage.

Examples:

Poking a finger in someone's chest

Pushing or shoving

Pushing, throwing, or kicking objects at others

Wrestling

Punching

Fighting

Attempting to hurt self (e.g., carving in own skin)

Level V – Using Violence toward People, with the Potential for Causing Serious Injury or Death

A youngster responds with a behavior that physically hurts others or self and produces long-lasting or permanent physical or psychological damage.

Examples:

Stalking

Bomb threats

Terrorism

Aggravated assault

Rape

Suicide

Murder

These five levels range in extremes from low-level behaviors like crying, whining, and teasing (Level I – noncompliance and/or making threatening statements or gestures) to the highest level, which involves acts of violence like physical assault, rape, and murder (Level V – using violence toward people, with the potential for causing serious injury or death). Movement along the continuum – from Level I to Level V – is characterized by an increase in the intensity and severity of the aggressive behaviors being displayed. For instance, the behaviors included in Level III (harming or killing animals) are more serious and severe than those that make up Level II (causing property damage).

(Keep in mind that Figure 1 contains examples of just a few of the behaviors in each level and is not an all-inclusive list of aggressive and violent behavior. These examples are offered as a general description of the kinds of aggressive and violent behaviors that characterize each level.)

This same type of continuum also applies to the aggressive behaviors within each level. For example, Level I (noncompliance and/or making threatening statements or gestures) behaviors like yelling or cursing – although extremely inappropriate – are not as serious or severe as making verbal threats to others or self.

Some children and adolescents who advance to the highest level of aggressive behaviors – Level V – do so in a sequential fashion, moving from one behavior to the next within a level, and then from one level to the next. Other kids, however, might suddenly move from using Level I aggressive behaviors like whining and teasing to a Level V act like assault or rape or murder. With these kids, there are few or no warning signs or clues that a youth is about to act in a highly aggressive or violent manner.

It is very important to remember that every child is different and each child's situation is unique. So – in the absence of any intervention – how slowly or quickly youth move from one level to the next (or from one aggressive behavior to the next within a level)

is highly individualized and depends on many factors in a child's life. The five levels are simply guidelines, an assessment tool that helps caregivers to more competently and accurately gauge the seriousness of a youth's aggression problem. This assessment will help them determine what course of action to take. The levels should not be used to label youngsters or to indicate that they are beyond help.

Most caregivers reading this book are probably caring for a youth (or a population of youngsters) who is displaying aggressive behaviors at higher levels on the continuum; this makes dealing with the youngster's severe behaviors more difficult and frustrating. Hang in there! There is hope; these youth can be helped. It is important for caregivers to realize that the first step in reducing aggression in youngsters is developing the ability to accurately recognize and evaluate the seriousness of a child's aggression problem. This gives caregivers a place to start – a base line – that can help them as they initially develop a plan for effective treatment, and later assess whether intervention strategies are working or need adjustment.

What Aggression Is Not: Anger and Assertiveness

The five levels of severity in aggression provide a strong foundation for understanding what aggressive behavior is, and the wide range of behaviors that make up aggression. However, it is equally important for caregivers to recognize that there are certain behaviors and instances that may on the surface appear to be aggressive, but in reality are not. Anger and assertiveness fall into this category.

Knowing what aggression is not enables parents and caregivers to distinguish between appropriate – even prosocial – behavior that should be praised and reinforced, and harmful, aggressive behavior that requires intervention. For example, a youth who "takes the bull by the horns" to accomplish a goal might be seen as being aggressive when, in fact, he or she is actually showing self-reliance, independence, and assertiveness. Knowledge of these differences will have a tremendous impact on how you deal with a youngster's behavior and the treatment strategies you develop and use with youth.

This section will discuss how anger and assertiveness are sometimes mistaken for aggression, and the factors that determine when anger and assertiveness cross over the line into aggression.

Aggression and Anger

Jason, a 10-year-old boy, walks into his bedroom and finds his prized baseball card collection strewn about the floor. Several cards are ripped and others have been smudged with a permanent marker.

Mary, Jason's 3-year-old stepsister, is standing with her back to Jason, coloring on one of Jason's favorite posters. Jason yells at Mary to stop; she drops the marker and runs out of the room. Instead of chasing after her, Jason stomps downstairs sobbing, and loudly tells his stepmother what happened. After talking with his stepmother for a few minutes, Jason is able to calm down. They agree that the ruined cards and poster will be replaced.

— ◆ —

Thirteen-year-old Tonya gets braces for her teeth. When she arrives at school the next day, she waits for someone to call her names or tell her how stupid and ugly she looks; she is ready to show everyone what happens if they "mess" with her. Few kids say anything. All the students know that Tonya might lash out at them, as she has many times in the past.

At lunch, Tommy, a new student, sits across from Tonya at a table. On a dare from some of the boys he wants to impress, Tommy takes a piece of tin foil from his lunch sack, puts it on his teeth, and flashes a huge grin at Tonya.

Tonya shouts, "Stop it you a------!" Suddenly, she picks up her lunch tray and throws it at Tommy, hitting him in the head. Then she climbs over the table and grabs Tommy's hair, trying to pull it out in clumps. Within seconds, both kids fall to the floor,

where Tonya starts to punch, kick, and bite Tommy. It takes three teachers to pull Tonya off Tommy, who ends up with a cut on his cheek, a swollen eye, and a bite mark on his forearm that requires stitches. As a result of the melee, Tonya is expelled from school; the fight is the last straw in a long list of incidents where Tonya directed aggressive and violent behavior toward classmates and staff.

— ◆ —

Anger is a feeling that all youngsters commonly experience during childhood and adolescence. Anger can be justified or unjustified. An example of justified anger would be a youngster who becomes angry when she finds out a friend lied to her. Unjustified anger is illustrated by a child who gets mad when told he can't have a piece of cake before dinner.

In the examples with Jason and Tonya, both kids were justified in feeling angry. Most youngsters would be mad if a special possession was destroyed or if someone teased and made fun of them. However, what sets these two youngsters apart is how they react and behave when they feel angry.

Jason's actions following his initial feelings of anger were appropriate, socially acceptable, and healthy ways for a 10-year-old to deal with what his sister did. The end result was that there were no serious aggressive behaviors, no one was hurt, and Jason was able to get his needs met by talking with his stepmother. Even though Jason was mad, he was still able to make a good decision to get an adult involved. In fact, Jason should receive a pat on the back from his stepmother for handling a potentially volatile situation in a constructive way. This would reinforce Jason's prosocial response and increase the likelihood that he will react the same way when he gets mad in the future.

On the other hand, Tonya's feelings of anger resulted in dangerous, antisocial, and violent behaviors. Her way of reacting to situations when she gets mad is to strike out in destructive and harmful ways. This results in many negative consequences, the most obvious being her expulsion from school.

10

Other consequences might include alienation from friends and teachers, and relationship problems with siblings and parents at home. Obviously, Tonya's use of high-level aggressive and violent behaviors when she is angry warrants immediate professional intervention.

Many kids have learned how to control their anger or express it appropriately; others have not, and respond with aggressive and violent behaviors. These are the kids who require intervention and help in learning new, more appropriate ways of handling situations where they become angry.

Whether anger is justified or not, youngsters must learn how to control their feelings and the behaviors they use to express them. One way caregivers can help kids learn to do this is by teaching them not to get angry when things don't go their way or they don't get what they want. When kids learn that they can control negative thoughts and feelings, they will be better able to control negative behaviors.

Aggression and Assertiveness

Janice is a 15-year-old student who earns excellent grades in all her classes. Her goal is to receive all "A's" during high school so she can earn a college scholarship. But Janice's teachers and classmates don't like her very much because she's so obnoxious.

Janice constantly bombards her teachers with mundane or irrelevant questions, or verbally challenges them on everything from simple class rules to grades she receives on assignments and tests. This always happens during class time and takes a lot of teaching time and attention away from the other students. Janice's teachers have asked her to come to them after class with questions and other issues, but Janice ignores their requests – she demands answers right then and there.

Janice's classmates are frustrated because she dominates the teacher's time. Once assignments and tests are handed back, Janice pesters other students about what grade they received, and constantly boasts about her high marks.

— ◆ —

Eleven-year-old Mark just moved into a new house with his foster parents and is trying to make friends with other kids in the neighborhood. For the last two weeks, Paul, the neighborhood bully has been "hassling" Mark whenever they are together with a group of kids from the area. Paul teases Mark about his thick glasses and constantly puts Mark down in front of others by calling him a "geek" or "dork."

When Paul isn't around, Mark gets along with almost all of the neighborhood kids. But when Paul is present, many of the other kids laugh at Paul's remarks and join in the teasing.

Mark finally decides to do something about Paul's continual harassment. One day after school, Mark goes over to Paul's house and asks Paul to stop making fun of him. At first, Paul laughs at Mark's request and tells him to "get lost." Mark is nervous and intimidated, but he calmly tells Paul that if the teasing doesn't stop right away, he will get their parents involved. Paul, afraid of what his mother might do, reluctantly agrees to leave Mark alone.

— ◆ —

Assertiveness is defined by Lange and Jakubowski (1976) as "...standing up for personal rights and expressing thoughts, feelings, and beliefs in *direct, honest,* and *appropriate* ways which do not violate another person's rights." This definition also applies to a situation where a person stands up for or defends another person (e.g., an older youth is teasing a younger child; another youngster steps in and asks the older youth to stop).

An integral part of assertiveness is respect. More specifically, this involves respect for one's own needs and rights and for the needs and rights of others. Assertiveness is not simply a way to get what one wants – it is a two-way street where the needs and rights of everyone involved are important.

Given the examples with Janice and Mark, many caregivers would maintain that both kids are being assertive because they are getting their needs met without harming anyone. However, there are significant differences in how each youth goes about solving the problems they have with others.

On the surface, Janice appears to be acting assertively; she is standing up for her rights and expressing her thoughts, feelings, and beliefs in direct and honest ways. But, she is not doing so in the appropriate manner that her teachers requested. In addition, Janice is violating the rights of her classmates because she ignores their need for help, attention, and instruction from the teacher. In fact, much of her behavior could be considered low-level forms of aggression (e.g., noncompliance, teasing, demanding statements, etc.) that require correction from her teachers and parents.

On the other hand, Mark demonstrates assertive behavior in resolving his issues with Paul, the neighborhood bully. He stands up for his rights and needs in a direct, honest, and appropriate way while also respecting Paul's rights and needs. How? Instead of asking Paul in front of the other kids to stop making fun of him, Mark goes to Paul's house to meet with him alone. This allows Paul to save face and avoid any embarrassment in front of his peers. Mark also gives Paul an opportunity to change his behavior by talking about getting their parents involved instead of simply telling the parents. Mark's assertive approach contributes to a favorable outcome. Lange and Jakubowski (1976) state that "...a by-product of responsible assertion is that people often do get what they want. Why? Because most people become cooperative when they are approached in a way which is both respectful of self and respectful of others."

Many times a youngster's behavior may appear assertive when it is actually inappropriate, or in some cases, aggressive. Again, the key question in determining whether a youth's behavior is assertive involves appropriate behavior and respecting rights: Is the youngster standing up for his or her rights and needs (or the rights and needs of another person) in honest and appropriate ways that also respect the rights of others? If the answer is "Yes," then the child is being assertive. If the answer is "No," then intervention is required to help the youth learn more responsible and acceptable ways of getting his or her needs met.

Is Aggression Ever Justified?

So far, we have defined aggression in strictly negative terms. Aggression in children and adolescents is a behavior that parents and caregivers want to either prevent or reduce as they teach kids prosocial and positive ways to solve problems or get what they want. There are times, however, when aggressive behavior is both appropriate and necessary. This "justified aggression" can include the use of verbal or physical force, and people most often resort to it in extreme situations where they must act to protect or defend themselves or others.

Consider this example: A young girl is walking home from school when a stranger (a man) in a car pulls up to the curb and asks her for directions. When the girl approaches the car, the man suddenly grabs her arm. She reacts by screaming, scratching his face, and eventually biting his hand. The stranger lets go and drives off as the girl runs to the safety of a nearby house.

In this example, the girl was probably thinking that the man was going to kidnap and possibly kill her. This thinking led to feelings of fear, which resulted in the aggressive behaviors of screaming, scratching, and biting. But because she was acting out of self-preservation and self-defense, her actions were justified and appropriate.

Would these same behaviors be justified if the girl attacked her mother because she wouldn't let the girl go to a movie with friends? Absolutely not. In this situation, the girl's thinking might be that her mom is always mean and never fair. This could lead to feelings of anger and frustration, which result in the aggressive behaviors of screaming, scratching, and biting. In this case, the girl's thoughts, feelings, and behaviors would not be justified, and she would likely earn severe negative consequences.

As we said earlier, justified aggression also can be used to protect others. For example, an intruder breaks into a house while a family is sleeping. The father wakes up, grabs a baseball bat, and hits the intruder with it. The father thought the intruder was going to hurt his family, he felt fear and anger, and responded with aggression. Obviously, the father's thoughts, feelings, and aggressive action were justified and appropriate because he was protecting himself and his family from harm.

While it is important to point out to parents and caregivers that children should be taught that they have the right to protect themselves or others by any means possible, we do want to stress that most aggression is undesirable and harmful. Obviously, children can choose to misuse this right, saying that they slugged a classmate on the playground because they felt threatened or in danger. In these situations, parents and caregivers have to make a judgment call about whether the child's behavior is justified or not, and respond accordingly.

Reactive Aggression and Proactive Aggression

During the last three years, 14-year-old Bobby has been arrested for shoplifting clothes and shoes at an athletic apparel store, vandalizing the house of a girl who refused to be his girlfriend, trespassing on school property, and stealing an expensive mountain bike from another youth at the local mall. At school, Bobby is considered a troublemaker and a behavior problem; many of his afternoons are spent in after-school detention – if he shows up. He constantly makes excuses and tries to sweet-talk his way out of detention and other negative consequences. When that doesn't work, he often gets angry and challenges his teachers. As a result, many of Bobby's teachers let him off the hook and dismiss any consequences because they don't want to deal with his temper tantrums. Big for his age, Bobby is taller and stronger than his classmates. Most students are afraid of him, and he uses his physical superiority to intimidate others, which allows him to get what he wants. Bobby teases his fellow classmates, threatens them, dominates them, laughs at them, and always seems to be fighting. The only friends he has are older boys who also are labeled as "troublemakers" and "bullies" by teachers and parents.

Bobby uses these same aggressive behaviors at home to get out of doing chores, homework, or any activity he doesn't like. His parents are fed up with him, and their attempts to punish Bobby for his negative behavior inevitably result in shouting matches. Bobby ends up winning these arguments by escalating his yelling and screaming to cursing, verbal threats, and physically aggressive posturing; eventually his parents give up and walk away. In the end, Bobby escapes any consequences from his parents for his inappropriate actions at home or school.

—— ◆ ——

Tina is an 11-year-old girl who recently was arrested for assaulting a teacher for the second time in 10 months. In the latest incident, Tina was arguing with her teacher over a detention she got for being late to class following lunch. (This was the third time in three days that Tina had been late.) Tina initially began making excuses and blamed another student for her tardiness; she refused to accept the detention and ignored her teacher's requests to calm down. Eventually, Tina started to curse, shout, and verbally threaten her teacher. When the teacher asked Tina to leave the classroom and report to the office, Tina "lost it" and shoved the teacher over a chair, then started to hit and kick her. Tina even tried to choke the teacher. The teacher suffered a gash on the back of her head and had to make a trip to the emergency room for stitches.

Other teachers describe Tina as "a bomb ready to explode." Most teachers ignore Tina's minor offenses for fear of having to deal with her explosive temper. Tina is an outcast at school and in her neighborhood. She overreacts to minor problems and is viewed as volatile and short-tempered. Other kids don't want to play with her because she might lash out at any time. Tina has been involved in many fights with both girls and boys in her neighborhood and at school. Usually, Tina doesn't start these fights, but she does escalate conflicts and doesn't try to avoid them.

Tina's parents are divorced and she lives with her mother. At home, Tina regularly punches and kicks her younger brother, two sisters, and mother.

—— ◆ ——

In these examples, Bobby and Tina share many common problems. Other kids don't like them and they have few, if any, friends. Teachers are frustrated with their constant outbursts and are growing weary of battling with them. And their relationships with their parents and siblings at home are in shambles. For both Bobby and Tina, one common destructive element is the major source of their difficulties: They both have learned that using aggressive behaviors is the most effective way to get what they want, escape trouble and negative consequences, or avoid something they don't want to do.

Despite this similarity, Tina and Bobby use aggression in different ways. In order to get his needs met, Bobby bullies and hassles others. In other words, Bobby initiates situations where he uses aggressive behaviors. Tina, on the other hand, responds with aggressive behaviors to the actions or behaviors of others. She loses control of her emotions and actions without thinking of the consequences and rapidly explodes in angry and hostile outbursts when an obstacle gets in her way. Dodge (1991) refers to these distinct types of aggressive behaviors as *proactive aggression* (Bobby) and *reactive aggression* (Tina).

Understanding and identifying which type of aggressive behavior a youth tends to use is an integral part of developing a strategy for teaching aggressive youth more appropriate responses to situations that frustrate, anger, or upset them. When parents and caregivers understand the "what" and "why" of proactive and reactive aggressive behavior, they are better able to cope with and help very difficult and frustrating children and adolescents.

Catching aggression when it is at lower levels, and becoming adept at recognizing the type of aggressive behavior a youth displays also enables caregivers to more accurately develop effective intervention strategies. This is important because, in many cases, using or choosing the wrong type of intervention may actually cause aggressive behavior to get worse.

This section will take a closer look at reactive and proactive aggression and how to identify each one.

Reactive Aggression

According to Dodge (1991), "…reactive aggression is displayed as anger or temper tantrums, with an appearance of being out of control."

These youngsters are bothered and upset by the actions and reactions of others, and respond in an emotionally charged manner. Often, parents and caregivers refer to these kids as "having a short fuse" because they can quickly go from being calm to being very angry over even minor issues, like receiving a simple "No" answer or earning a small consequence for a negative behavior.

Some of these youngsters enjoy teasing other kids, but they don't like to be teased. They tend to misread situations and respond with quick and frequent temper outbursts. Other kids usually are afraid of them and view them as unpredictable.

Other reactive aggressive kids are explosive. They frequently have faulty thinking patterns and are quick to react to what they perceive as a hostile world. They are very sensitive to teasing and ridicule. When they can't avoid conflict, they often escalate it by using verbal and physical aggression.

Youngsters who use aggression reactively are unable to control their actions when they become angry, frustrated, and fearful. They are like the 2-year-old child in a restaurant who becomes angry and throws a tantrum because she can't have something she wants. That may be a normal and common response for most 2-year-olds, but is it socially unacceptable and inappropriate for an older child or adolescent?

Reactive aggressive kids tend to explode with high levels of aggressive and, at times, violent behavior. They don't typically move through the five levels of severity in aggression in a sequential or logical fashion, but usually proceed directly to more severe types of aggression like yelling, cursing, verbal threats, punching, or fighting.

Generally speaking, peers and classmates don't like these youngsters, and they can be a tremendous source of frustration for parents and caregivers because no one knows when they might erupt. These kids can be outgoing and gregarious or quiet and passive, but their aggressive response to feelings of anger, frustration, or fear is the same: It's unpredictable – even to the youngster – and laden with emotion.

Proactive Aggression

According to Dodge (1991), "Proactive aggression occurs usually in the form of object acquisition, bullying, or dominance of a peer." Instead of *responding* aggressively to conflict with others (reactive aggression), kids who use proactive aggression tend to *initiate* aggressive acts. Caregivers often refer to them as "manipulators" or "bullies." Aggression in these youngsters is more thought out and serves a purpose: It helps them reach a goal.

Many of these youngsters are known for "starting trouble," and are seen by other kids as bullies. They constantly tease, shove, call people names, etc., and often start fights for no apparent reason. Generally, they do poorly in school, both academically and socially.

Some youngsters who are proactive aggressive have learned to get their needs met by "setting up" others. They like to argue, threaten, and use other aggressive behaviors in order to get people to give in to their demands. They don't get along well with others and like to intimidate them.

Over time, proactive aggressive youth learn that they can get what they want by using aggressive behaviors. In fact, because their aggressive behavior is more cognitively oriented and calculating, these youth don't necessarily have to be angry or upset. With proactive aggression, hostile and inappropriate behavior is a harmful instrument for achieving goals, much like a construction worker uses a wrecking ball to destroy a building.

Children who use proactive aggression are apt to move through the five levels of severity in aggression in a more sequential, orderly manner. The tendency is to begin with lower-level aggressive behaviors and escalate to higher-level behaviors if a particular aggressive act is no longer achieving the desired results. For example, if a youngster finds that whining or complaining isn't enough to get out of doing chores at home, she will "turn up the heat" so to speak, resorting to more severe behaviors like yelling and cursing. Over time – without intervention – these kids might up the ante to the highest levels of aggression, like physically harming others or themselves (Level IV) or using violence toward people, with the potential for causing death (Level V).

Proactive aggressive children and adolescents tend to use the aggressive behaviors that have worked in the past with a particular individual or in a particular situation. Once these kids learn what level of aggression helps them accomplish their goal, they frequently begin at that level in every subsequent interaction that involves conflict. For instance, a youth may begin an argument with a parent by immediately using verbal threats or throwing objects; during a conflict with a teacher or a coach, however, that same child might use lower-level aggressive behaviors like noncompliance, whining, or crying.

Younger proactive aggressive kids are not necessarily disliked by their peers and classmates. However, as these kids get older, other children begin to see them in a more negative light. Like reactive aggressive kids, the personalities of proactive aggressive youngsters can range from outgoing and sociable to quiet and passive. So, when attempting to distinguish proactive aggressive youth from reactive aggressive youth, the key question involves *intent:* Is the child deliberately using aggression as a tool to serve a purpose or meet a goal?

Dodge (1991) states: "All behaviors have aspects of reaction and proaction, in that one

15

can make guesses regarding the precipitants as well as the functions of all behaviors." This is true for aggressive behavior. In extreme cases, it is much easier for parents and caregivers to distinguish between proactive and reactive aggression by looking at whether or not a child is angry and by determining the function of the aggressive behavior. On the other hand, the task of identification is more difficult with kids who are on the fringes. In either situation, it is important for parents and caregivers to accurately identify which type of aggression pattern a youngster is using so that responsible, effective intervention and treatment can be developed.

Bullying

Aaron, a sophomore, is feared by most of the students in his high school – and he likes it that way. Being taller and stronger than most of the other kids, Aaron is the only underclassman to make the varsity football team, and he will probably be a starting player. The coaches praise Aaron, a linebacker on defense, for his ferocious play and brutal hits.

Aaron doesn't leave this "football" behavior on the playing field. In school and in his neighborhood, Aaron uses his physical superiority to make others do what he wants. He thoroughly enjoys badgering and "shaking down" smaller kids for money or other possessions. For example, Aaron recently threatened to "kick the s--- out" of a younger boy in his neighborhood if the boy didn't give his portable CD player to Aaron. The boy handed it over because he knew from past experience that Aaron wouldn't hesitate to follow through with his threat. The boy was terrified and didn't tell an adult what happened because Aaron threatened to hurt the boy if he told anyone.

For fun, Aaron often intimidates other kids into doing things that are degrading and humiliating. For example, during lunch period one day he tried to force another male student to drink a mixture of milk and urine. When the boy refused, Aaron grabbed the boy's hair, wrestled him to the floor, and poured the concoction into the boy's mouth. No one – including the victim – reported this to a teacher because they were afraid that Aaron would get them for "squealing."

— ◆ —

In schools and neighborhoods around the world, wherever there are children, there are bullies. Kids like Aaron rule over and terrorize their victims mercilessly, and more often than not, get away with it. Why? Because victims of bullies and witnesses fear that the bully will "get" them if they tell an adult. So, victims go on suffering in silence as they are repeatedly hassled and tormented.

Bullying is defined by Olweus (1996) as "aggressive behavior or intentional 'harm-doing,' which is carried out repeatedly and over time in an interpersonal relationship characterized by an imbalance of power." Bullying "…often occurs without apparent provocation" and includes negative actions that "…can be carried out by physical contact, by words, or in other ways, such as making faces or mean gestures, and intentional exclusion from a group." Additionally, one of the goals of bullying is acquiring possessions – money, cigarettes, alcohol, and other things a bully values (Olweus, 1996). In sum, a bully consciously, deliberately, and repeatedly uses aggression to get what he or she wants from other youngsters who have difficulty defending themselves either physically or emotionally from the harassment. Bullying, therefore, is considered a form of proactive aggression.

Studies on bullying show that youth who are younger and weaker are victimized most often, and that the bully-victim relationship tends to last a long time unless there is some sort of intervention from parents or caretakers. Also, bullies and their victims usually are boys. However, there is a good deal of bullying that goes on among girls. One big difference between boy and girl bullies is that boys use physical force or tactics (e.g., pushing, kicking or tripping, punching, etc.) while girls tend to use more subtle forms of harassment like "…slandering, spreading of rumors, intentional exclusion from the group, and manipulation of friendship relations"

16

(Olweus, 1996). These subtle forms of bullying, according to Olweus (1996), are "more difficult to detect for adults."

How can parents and caregivers determine if a child they live with or care for is a bully? What are some of the characteristics of bullying that parents and caregivers should be aware of that would help them identify a problem? Olweus's research (1996) provides some answers to these questions:

♦ Bullies engage in aggressive and violent acts **in order to get something.** So, much of their behavior originates from a strong desire to obtain things or items that they feel they need or want.

♦ Bullies have **a positive attitude toward aggression** and violence. They enjoy the physical and emotional pain they inflict on others and won't hesitate to use intimidating and harassing behaviors.

♦ A strong **need to control and dominate** others – kids and adults – drives a bully's behavior.

♦ Bullies are **impulsive.** If they see something they want, they go after it without thinking about how their aggressive actions affect others or even the consequences to themselves.

♦ A bully has **little, if any, empathy** for his or her victims. Bullies simply don't care about the devastating impact their behavior can have on other people's lives.

♦ Contrary to popular belief, bullies **do not suffer from low self-esteem.** Surprisingly, the opposite is true: Bullies have little anxiety and are very secure in their identity.

♦ There is an **imbalance of power** between a bully and his or her victim. A typical victim is unable to defend himself or herself either physically or emotionally from a bully's harassment.

♦ Bullies who engage in extremely violent acts (e.g., assault, rape, murder, etc.) have **easy access to a deadly weapon,** like a knife or a gun.

Whatever form bullying takes – from simple verbal harassment to physical violence – it creates a harmful situation for both the bully and the victim. Children and adolescents who learn to rely on the use of force to get what they want will fail in a society where positive, appropriate social interaction between people is a key to success. In extreme cases, this failure can include alienation, criminal activity and incarceration, and an absence of meaningful relationships. For the victim, there is the immediate fear, humiliation, and pain of being singled out for abuse, as well as possible long-lasting effects like loss of self-confidence or a feeling of inferiority. Some victims of bullies also tend to become or remain victims in other areas of their lives as they mature.

As with any form of aggression, bullying demands immediate intervention. In later chapters, we will discuss treatment approaches and strategies for working with bullies and youth who use other forms of proactive aggression.

What We Know: A Summary of Aggression and Violence Studies

Aggression and violence have been well-studied by many researchers. The focus of their work has been wide and varied, involving the diverse issues that affect the development of aggressive and violent behavior during infancy, childhood, and adolescence. Rolf Loeber (1997) has put together a comprehensive piece that summarizes the body of excellent research in this area.

The information included in this section is intended to help round out and give caregivers a fuller picture of aggression and violence in children and adolescents. A summary of the more pertinent and interesting information and findings is provided here:

♦ During infancy (birth to one year old), boys are more likely to show forms of anger than girls. However, neither sex yet displays aggressive behaviors, other than rage and frustration, which are typical for infants.

17

♦ Aggressive behaviors, typically in the form of temper tantrums directed at adults and other children, begin at age 2 or 3. There is no noticeable difference between boys and girls at this age regarding the frequency of aggressive incidents.

♦ From ages 3 through 6 years, the difference in the level of aggressive behavior between boys and girls becomes more pronounced. Typically, males display higher levels of physically aggressive behavior than girls. Girls in this age range tend to use lower levels of aggressive behavior like crying, whining, excluding others from the group, gossiping, and so on.

♦ Most girls and many boys show an overall decrease in aggressive behaviors toward peers and adults and an increase in the use of interpersonal skills between the ages of 6 and 12 years. Only a small percentage of boys are unable to control their aggressive tendencies. However, both sexes frequently use aggressive behavior with siblings during this period. There also is the appearance of behaviors like cruelty toward others or animals. The emergence of these behaviors can signal the possible development of mental health problems such as Conduct Disorder or Oppositional Defiant Disorder, or more severe aggression problems.

♦ A number of changes regarding aggression occur during adolescence and young adulthood. These include:

• Aggression tends to increase in severity and involves more hostile acts toward others that cause serious mental, emotional, or physical damage, or death. This can be attributed to three things: Youngsters are physically stronger; there is a higher use of deadly weapons in confrontations; and it is easy for youngsters to obtain deadly weapons.

• Peer groups have a strong influence on youngsters, and a group as a whole tends to use aggression or violence (e.g., hassling a younger child to give up a possession or causing property damage to a school).

• The lure of gangs becomes stronger. Youngsters who join gangs have greater access to deadly weapons and are more likely to engage in severe forms of aggressive and violent acts.

• Adult-child conflict increases during this period. Kids are getting physically stronger, and aggressive youth are more likely to hit or physically harm an adult.

• Conflicts between boys and girls increase. Girls have more conflicts with boys than boys have with girls. This creates more aggression between the sexes, and as dating begins, aggressive and violent acts like physical assault or rape are more likely to occur.

• Some youngsters become sexually active and some have children of their own. Youngsters who become parents may begin abusing their own children and/or partners.

♦ The age of onset for aggressive behaviors gradually increases with each level of aggression. More specifically, behaviors included in the lowest level of aggression (Level I) typically begin at about age 3. Level II, Level III, and Level IV aggressive behaviors usually start to emerge around age 10, while behaviors at Level V – using violence toward people, with the potential for causing death – often begin at about age 11.

♦ Physical aggression (e.g, hitting, kicking, punching, etc.) is more likely to occur early in life, but the prevalence of such behavior decreases during adolescence. However, the use of serious violence (e.g., aggravated assault, rape, suicide, murder, etc.) tends to increase during adolescence.

♦ Youngsters who begin to use aggressive behavior early in life are much more likely to engage in severe forms of aggression and violence later in life. Several researchers have found that most violent adults involved in their studies also were aggressive when they were young.

◆ Youngsters whose parents report that their children have difficult temperaments are more likely to develop aggression problems.

◆ There are several cognitive factors that can promote aggression in children and adolescents, and hinder a youth's ability to maintain self-control during times of upset or crisis. These include:

- Low intelligence and academic problems.

- Difficulty paying and maintaining attention.

- Inability to generate solutions to problems or conflict in a nonaggressive manner.

- Misinterpreting or misreading social cues from others. Aggressive kids tend to think others are responding to them with an aggressive intent, when in fact that is not the case. This misinterpretation tends to elicit an aggressive response from the youngster.

- Exposure to a multitude of conflicts and aggression in the child's environment. This can lead to a preoccupation with aggression that increases the likelihood that a youth will use the antisocial behaviors he or she sees being used by others around him or her. In fact, overexposure to aggression and violence can dramatically influence a youngster's perception of the use of hostile behaviors; over time, he or she actually begins to view the use of these behaviors in a favorable light.

◆ Family factors can influence and promote the development of aggression and violence in youngsters. Some of these include:

- Insecure attachment relationships between children and their mothers during infancy, which can lead to behavior problems.

- Parental disciplinary practices that include coercive interactions, physical punishment or unreasonably punitive discipline, and physical abuse.

- Single-parent homes, where children are more likely to develop aggressive and violent tendencies.

◆ Highly aggressive children are rejected by their peers as early as age 6. As adolescents, these same kids do have friends, but the friends usually are other aggressive or deviant peers.

◆ Neighborhoods where aggression and violence are commonplace can significantly influence the development of aggressive and violent behaviors in kids. Further, this influence can lead children to adopt various levels of aggressive and violent behavior at an earlier age.

◆ Patterson (1990) found that girls who are highly aggressive also tend to be depressed.

Despite being well-researched, aggression and violence remain complicated issues. The information presented in this section is extremely valuable in helping caregivers quickly identify the signals that indicate that a child is learning or developing aggressive or violent tendencies. Caregivers must heed these warning signs and begin developing a plan to steer youth back to the road to success.

Summary

Just as a doctor must make an accurate diagnosis to heal a patient, caregivers must be able to accurately diagnose a youngster's behavioral or emotional problems in order to develop an effective Treatment Plan. This is especially true with aggression. The more knowledge caregivers have about what aggression is and what it is not, the more proficient they will be in identifying a youngster's level of aggression and the forms of aggression the child tends to use. Ultimately, this enhances the quality of treatment and increases the chances of helping a child overcome his or her aggression problem.

CHAPTER 2
Why Are Kids Aggressive?

How does aggressive and violent behavior become part of a youngster's life? When and where do aggression and violence begin to develop in children and adolescents? Is it "nature" or "nurture?" The classic debate of whether biology (nature) or environment (nurture) has a greater impact on a child's development has dominated the landscape of this issue – and numerous other issues in the field of psychology – for many years. However, choosing one theory over the other as the end-all answer is both shortsighted and irresponsible. The only hope for gaining a solid foothold on understanding this complex problem and providing effective treatment is to adopt a multidimensional view. That involves taking into account the importance and value of various approaches to helping youth overcome their aggression problems, and not confining treatment possibilities to only one modality.

Recently, researchers have begun to identify the significant and relevant role that biology, environment, and cognitive and perceptual processes play in the development of aggression and violence. Grisso (1996) states: "Each of the three perspectives has different pieces of a map that lead to the destination we all seek." This means that just as there is no single cause for the development of aggression and violence in youngsters, there also is no one definitive explanation or treatment approach.

Boys Town subscribes to this philosophy. Boys Town believes that aggression and other antisocial behaviors are learned and evolve from the many influences in a youngster's environment (e.g., parents, siblings, friends, other adults and family members), and from faulty cognitive and perceptual processes (i.e., thoughts and feelings). That is why the Boys Town Teaching Model incorporates a treatment approach that includes teaching troubled youngsters alternative appropriate behaviors to replace old, negative behaviors. In addition, Boys Town helps aggressive and violent kids correct flawed cognitive and perceptual patterns and the impact that they have on behaviors. Finally, it is important to note that Boys Town believes that biological interventions (e.g., psychotropic medications) can be an important piece of the puzzle when developing effective and therapeutic treatment plans for aggressive youngsters.

The concepts for this treatment philosophy are deeply rooted in research and theories on the causes of aggression in children. To effectively work with youth in your care, it is important to understand why youngsters sometimes explode in antagonistic, aggressive, and even violent ways toward themselves and others. Caregivers who are familiar with the various theories on aggression and violence are more likely to provide effective treatment that can help youth change these negative behaviors. Effective treatment also stems from a good understanding of the origins of a youth's negative behavior and why and how it continues to be reinforced. This is especially important when teaching youth alternative ways to calmly and rationally deal with stressful or adverse situations. When caregivers take the time to do their "homework" on these issues, they can more easily identify problems and possible solutions, which results in better care for the youth.

In order to provide some necessary insight on this issue, this chapter will focus on the findings of Gerald Patterson and Nicholas Long, two researchers whose extensive work has greatly influenced the strategies and teaching techniques Boys Town has refined for working with aggressive and violent youth. Both men have developed respected theories that seek to explain why youth respond to conflict in aggressive and violent ways, and how caregivers can effectively work with these youth. The two main theories we will be exploring are Patterson's *Coercion Process* and Long's *Conflict Cycle*. There also will be a brief discussion of the biological factors that can affect the development of aggressive behavior in children and adolescents.

The Coercion Process – Patterson

Coercion refers to the use of one or more aggressive behaviors or acts by a youth in response to the behavior of another person who generally is an authority figure (e.g., mother, father, teacher, foster parent, or other caregiver). The authority figure then responds to the youth's aggressive behavior in one of two ways, labeled by Patterson (1982) as *escape conditioning* or *negative synchronicity*. The end result of both types of responses is the same: The youth's aggressive behavior is reinforced. Over time, the youth is trained to use aggressive behavior whenever he or she is confronted with conflict because this behavior usually gets the youth what he or she wants. This cycle of reinforcing negative or aggressive youth behavior through counterproductive authority responses is called the *Coercion Process*.

Socially skilled youth have learned to use appropriate behaviors to resolve negative or unpleasant social situations. However, children who do not learn socially appropriate behaviors will develop coping mechanisms to overcome these deficiencies. Children who have not been taught appropriate social skills learn to use the response that works best for them in a given situation. Children are extremely tuned in to their social environment and learn to match their behavior to inadequate parental discipline and responses, lack of structure, poor problem-solving abilities, and what they see as "hassles" from adults.

The following sections explain the concepts of escape conditioning and negative synchronicity, and present examples of each.

Escape Conditioning

In this scenario, the authority figure gives in and submits to the youth's coercive attack or aggressive behavior. Thus, the unpleasant interaction abruptly ends and the authority figure escapes any further unpleasant or painful exchanges with the youth. Unfortunately, this only reinforces the youth's aggressive behavior by teaching him or her that the authority figure will withdraw his or her aversive behaviors if the child's behavior escalates beyond "tolerable" limits.

Example – A mother scolds her son for staying out well past his curfew. The son responds by screaming at his mother, "Stop your d--- b-------. I don't know what the h--- your problem is!" The son screams these verbally aggressive statements (coercion) at his mother so she will stop scolding him. The mother immediately ceases the scolding and walks away, avoiding any further conflict with the son. The son does not receive a consequence for staying out past his curfew, and has now learned that he can stop or escape his mother's scolding by becoming verbally aggressive.

Negative Synchronicity

In this situation, the authority figure immediately responds with aversive behavior when a youth engages in an aggressive behavior. The coercive youth, in turn, escalates the intensity of his or her aggressive behavior until he or she "out-punishes" the authority figure. Eventually, the youth's aggressive behavior intensifies to the point where the authority figure concedes and ends the interaction. Again, the authority figure's response reinforces the youth's aggressive behavior.

Patterson showed that members of clinic-referred families were often entrenched in this type of behavior-reaction cycle, and were roughly twice as likely as members of "normal" families to respond in this combative interaction style.

Example – A father comes home after a long day's work and begins scolding his son for not taking out the trash. The son screams at his father, "You take that s--- out yourself!" The father angrily shouts back, "I run this house and if you know what's good for you, you'll do what I tell you! Go take that d--- trash out! Now!" The son increases the intensity and severity of his aggressive behavior by shouting back at his father, cursing, and kicking the leg of the kitchen table. In turn, the father threatens to "ground" the son.

Upping the ante, the son responds by aggressively walking toward his father with clenched fists, angrily shouting, "I'll do what I want. If you don't like it, I'll kick your a--!" At this point, the father backs away and leaves the room, ending the hostile exchange. The son has learned that by escalating the intensity and severity of his aggressive behaviors, he can avoid taking out the trash and eventually stop his father's aversive behaviors.

Patterson's research helps to explain many of the clinical problems, including children's aggressive and violent behavior, that caregivers see today in increasing numbers. Coercive children respond to authority figures by trying to "out-punish" them. In some families, these aggressive behaviors are reinforced so often that the coercive child actually runs the family and controls the social setting. If these youth do not receive consequences for their aggressive behaviors, they continue to use them whenever someone confronts them. These behaviors eventually spill over into interactions with others – family members, teachers, and other kids – whom the coercive child tries to out-punish or out-intimidate. The result usually is a child who depends solely on negative, aggressive, or aversive behaviors to get his or her needs met or to interact with others.

The Conflict Cycle – Long

Long believes that a crisis has its root cause in an unresolved incident, and is the product of a youth's stress that is kept alive by the actions and the reactions of others. The incident arouses strong emotions in the youth and others who are involved, and even a minor disagreement can spiral into a major crisis.

When a youth's feelings are aroused by stress, the youth learns to behave in ways that shield him or her from painful feelings. Others (parents, teachers, peers) perceive the youth's behavior as negative, and they respond in a negative fashion toward the youth. This response produces additional stress and the youth again reacts in an inappropriate manner to protect himself or herself from further hurtful feelings. If unbroken, this spiraling action-reaction cycle dominates interactions the youth has with others. This process is called the *Conflict Cycle.*

The Conflict Cycle follows this pattern: The first step is a stressful event (e.g., frustration, failure, rejection) that triggers a troubled youth's irrational or negative beliefs (e.g., "Nothing good ever happens to me!"; "Adults are out to get me!"). Negative thoughts determine and trigger negative feelings and anxieties, which drive the youth's aggressive behavior. The aggressive behaviors (e.g., yelling, screaming, threatening, sarcasm, refusing to speak, and so on) incite others, who not only pick up the youth's negative feelings but also frequently

mirror the youth's negative behaviors. This aversive reaction increases the youth's stress, triggers more intense feelings, and drives more aggressive behavior. The youth's behavior leads the people around him or her to feel even more anger and frustration. This cycle continues until it escalates into a no-win power struggle. Wood and Long (1991) say: "Logic, caring, and compassion are lost, and the only goal is to win the power struggle."

In the end, the youth's irrational beliefs (e.g., "Nothing good ever happens to me!"; "Adults are out to get me!") that started the Conflict Cycle sequence are reinforced, and the youth has no reason to change or alter his or her irrational beliefs and aggressive behaviors.

The following is an example of the Conflict Cycle. (The cycle is illustrated in Figure 1.)

Figure 1
Conflict Cycle

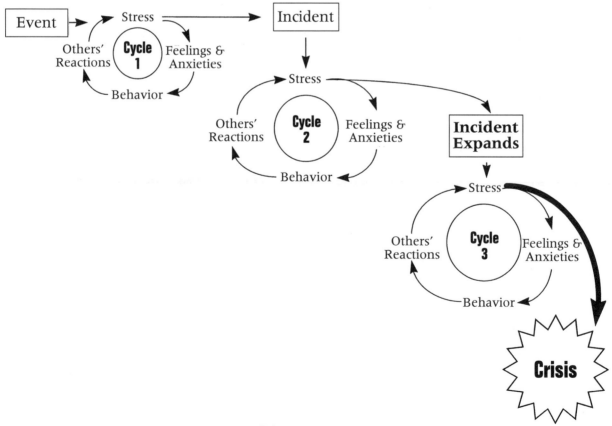

Example – A youth is absent from school and misses a math test. Because the youth doesn't have a legitimate written excuse for the absence the next day, the teacher tells her she must take the math exam after school or receive an "F." (*Event* creating *Stress – Cycle 1 Begins*). The youth is frustrated because she does not want to stay after school and miss play practice (*Feelings/Anxieties*). She makes several excuses, attempting to talk her way out of staying after school to take the test (*Negative Behavior*). The teacher tells the student to be quiet, accept the situation, and start her current math assignment (*Others' Reactions* creating *More Stress – Cycle 2 Begins*). Becoming agitated (*Feelings/ Anxieties)*, the youth begins to yell at the teacher about being unfair (*Negative Behavior*). The teacher responds by sarcastically saying, "You probably skipped school yesterday anyway. You're lucky I don't just give you an 'F.'" (*Others' Reactions* creating *More Stress – Cycle 3 Begins*). Embarrassed in front of her classmates (*Feelings/Anxieties*), the youth begins to scream and curse at the teacher (*Negative Behavior*). The teacher angrily yells at the youth to report to the office, which will result in a call home (*Others' Reactions* creating *More Stress – Crisis*). Now the youth is extremely angry and frustrated over the additional consequence. She knocks her books to the floor, throws a pen at the teacher, and tips over her desk before leaving the classroom and walking out of school.

Biology

As mentioned earlier, biology is another important and valuable perspective to consider, both when evaluating a child's aggression problem and determining if any biological interventions (e.g., psychotropic medication, chemical dependency program, and others) might be effective in the child's overall Treatment Plan.

Reiss and Roth (1993) cite three biological factors that may play a role in the development of aggressive and violent behavior in youth.

- **Genetics** – The contention is that the presence of certain genes might cause some youngsters to be predisposed to aggression and violence. Even though rapid advances are being made in research that studies the connection between genetics and behavior, Grisso (1996) states that, at the present time, "...there is no credible evidence for a link between genes and aggressive or violent behavior."

- **Neurobiological processes** – Reiss and Roth (1993) describe these processes as "the complex electrical (neurophysiological) and chemical (neurochemical and neuroendocrine) activities in specific brain regions that underlie all externally observable behaviors." Simply put, some children may behave the way they do because certain electrical and chemical activities in the brain are not occurring normally or correctly. In these instances, treatment might be improved through the use of pharmacological interventions (psychotropic medications) that may correct these chemical and electrical activities. But Reiss and Roth (1993) state: "To date, no known neurobiological patterns are precise and specific enough to be considered reliable markers..." for aggressive and violent behaviors. There are probably hundreds of neurotransmitters, and presently, there is knowledge of only a handful. As in the field of genetics, research in this area is rapidly progressing and showing exciting potential.

- **Alcohol and drug use or abuse** – Much research has been done in the area of how alcohol and drug use affect behavior. Many studies show that there is a strong correlation between long-term, heavy alcohol use and aggressive and violent behavior. Also, the chronic use and abuse of certain psychoactive drugs (e.g., amphetamines, LSD, PCP, and others) have been linked to aggressive behavior patterns and unusual hostile or violent outbursts.

Summary

The Boys Town Teaching Model's theoretical foundation and subsequent treatment philosophy is based on the belief that aggressive and violent behaviors are learned and evolve from the many influences in a youth's environment. Aggression also can develop as a result of faulty cognitive and perceptual processes (i.e., thoughts and feelings). In addition, Boys Town recognizes the important role biological factors (e.g., genetics, neurobiological processes, and alcohol and drug use or abuse) can play in aggression, and the importance of considering these factors during treatment planning.

In order for caregivers to develop effective treatment plans for the children in their care, it is important that they have a basic understanding of the wide range of research and theory regarding the causes of aggression and violence. This understanding enhances caregivers' abilities to identify problems and find solutions.

The researchers whose work has greatly influenced Boys Town's treatment approach with aggressive youth are Gerald Patterson, Mary Wood, and Nicholas Long. Patterson's Coercive Process and Wood's and Long's Conflict Cycle provide insight into the origins and causes of aggressive behavior in children, and how it can be reinforced through interactions involving the children and authority figures.

CHAPTER 3

How Boys Town Reduces Aggression

When Father Edward J. Flanagan founded Boys Town in 1917, he started a revolution in the way America cares for her troubled children. His ideas about surrounding kids with love and teaching them how to be productive citizens were far ahead of their time, and set new standards for child care.

Over the years, Boys Town has helped thousands of children change their lives for the better. And as the problems kids face have become more complex and difficult, Boys Town has changed to meet those new challenges. The ability to develop treatment approaches that are innovative and effective, yet still have as their foundation the old-fashioned love and respect championed by Father Flanagan, has always been one of Boys Town's strengths. From that strength and the desire to remain on the cutting edge of child-care technology came the Boys Town Teaching Model.

The Boys Town Teaching Model is at the heart of every Boys Town treatment program. The result of extensive research and decades of experience working with children, the Model has evolved and been improved to

meet the unique problems that today's kids and caregivers face. It is a proven, successful model of care that is effective in diverse settings and situations with a variety of youth populations. Replicated at Boys Town sites across the country and in a variety of child-care programs and school systems, the Model provides a practical approach to helping troubled kids learn new prosocial ways to solve problems and get their needs met.

The Boys Town Teaching Model comprises three main qualities: teaching social skills, building relationships, and empowering kids through teaching self-control. These components make the Model especially effective when working with aggressive children and adolescents. Social skill instruction gives kids new, positive behaviors that can replace aggressive behaviors. As youth become proficient in using new skills, they are better able to identify the causes of aggression and control their feelings and behaviors. This sense of empowerment helps kids understand and feel confident that they can make good decisions on their own. Finally, relationship-building is important because it helps caregivers create and develop a genuine bond with kids. Kids are more receptive to teaching if they believe that someone genuinely cares about them. They also learn that getting along with other people is a more positive experience than using force or intimidation, and that respecting the rights of others is the only way to earn real respect.

In this chapter, we will discuss the components of the Boys Town Teaching Model and how they are effective in Boys Town's approach to treating aggression. In addition, we will present a summary of Boys Town's research and data that shows that exposure to and treatment provided through the Boys Town Teaching Model results in reduced aggression in kids. In following chapters, we will explain the Teaching Interactions (Corrective Teaching, Crisis Teaching, Effective Praise, Proactive Teaching) that are part of the Model's treatment approach.

Overview of Social Skill Instruction

The philosophy of the Boys Town Teaching Model regarding social skill instruction is that youth who use aggressive or violent behaviors (and other antisocial behaviors) do so because they have not learned, or have learned not to use, positive, appropriate ways to deal with situations that arouse feelings of anger, frustration, and disappointment. The only way they know how to respond effectively to these unpleasant feelings is by lashing out in hostile and, at times, violent ways. In order to help these kids overcome their aggression problem, the Model focuses on teaching and strengthening alternative prosocial skills or behaviors. Simply put, aggressive kids are taught new skills – or ways to behave – that allow them to get what they want or need and solve problems in peaceful, productive, and socially acceptable ways.

In the Boys Town Teaching Model, social, academic, and vocational skills, as well as spiritual values, are taught in a "family-style" treatment setting through proactively teach-ing at neutral times, reinforcing positive behavior as it occurs, helping kids practice and rehearse new skills, correcting inappropriate behavior in a positive style, and helping youth learn to use alternative appropriate behaviors when they face crisis situations.

According to Combs and Slaby (1977), a social skill can be defined as "the ability to interact with others in a given social context in specific ways that are socially acceptable or valued and, at the same time, personally beneficial, mutually beneficial, or beneficial primarily to others." Thus, social skills are sets of behaviors that can be modified to fit the demands of the social context and particular situation. In addition, using these skills benefits the person who uses them as well as others.

During the entire treatment planning process, it is extremely important for caregivers to view each child individually. This is especially true when determining what social skills are the most appropriate and therapeutic for each youth. For example, even though two kids may have aggression as their primary treatment issue, each youth may need to learn a different set of skills in order to best meet his or her treatment goals.

Boys Town has identified and developed 182 skills as part of its Social Skill Curriculum. These skills help caregivers address a wide variety of youth issues at all levels, from minor school- or home-related problems to more serious problems like aggression, delinquency, depression, and suicide. These four types of skills – basic, intermediate, advanced, and complex – give kids alternative positive behaviors to use instead of the negative behaviors that get them in trouble.

Typically, when youngsters are first introduced to social skill instruction they need to learn the most basic skills (e.g., *Following Instructions, Accepting Consequences, Accepting "No" Answers*, etc.). This lays a foundation for learning more complex skills (e.g., *Expressing Feelings Appropriately, Assertiveness, Spontaneous Problem-Solving*, etc.). Many times, caregivers will need to gradually shape a youth's behavior in order to teach more difficult skills. Caregivers can begin this process by first patiently teaching the basic social skills. Once a child demonstrates proficiency using a certain skill or set of skills, caregivers can introduce and begin teaching the next appropriate, more complex skill. Shaping can sometimes be a slow, arduous process for caregivers and youth, but it is necessary if a youth is to overcome his or her problems.

For some kids, appropriately and consistently using social skills is difficult because it involves an immensely complex chain of rapidly occurring interpersonal events. For example, some aggressive youth suffer from mental health disorders like Conduct Disorder or Oppositional Defiant Disorder, which can dramatically interfere with and disrupt their emotional and cognitive functioning. Correctly using the right skill at the right time can be a daunting task for these youngsters. They have a difficult time organizing and blending their behaviors into smooth-flowing interactions with others, particularly when they are under stress or in crisis. Since each youth has his or her own unique learning style, caregivers must be able and willing to adjust their teaching techniques, vocabulary, and interpersonal behaviors to best meet each youngster's needs.

Other factors like the age and developmental level of the youngster, severity and intensity of the youth's behaviors, and the length of time a youth has been exposed to social skill instruction play an important role in a caregiver's decisions on which social skills to teach as part of treatment. Often, the success or failure of a youth's Treatment Plan hinges on these decisions. Once caregivers identify and prioritize the appropriate skills for treatment, they can use the various Teaching Interactions (e.g., Proactive Teaching, Effective Praise, Corrective Teaching, and Crisis Teaching) to reinforce and teach youth new prosocial ways of responding to others, and to situations that have caused them problems in the past.

All 182 curriculum skills and the steps to each skill are presented in Boys Town's manual, *Teaching Social Skills to Youth: A Curriculum for Child-Care Providers*. (Also see Boys Town's book, *Treating Youth with DSM-IV Disorders: The Role of Social Skill Instruction*. This book contains a series of charts that list social skills to teach to children and adolescents who require treatment for specific DSM-IV disorders.) The curriculum can be easily integrated into a variety of settings (e.g., natural home environment, classroom, emergency shelter care program, group home residential program, psychiatric treatment program, and others) for troubled kids with a variety of problems.

The Teaching Interactions that form the cornerstone of treatment planning and active intervention at Boys Town will be presented later in this book. Also, the Appendix, "Social Skills for Aggressive Youth," in the back of this book contains skills from the Boys Town Social Skill Curriculum that are specific, appropriate, and therapeutic for treating kids who tend to use reactive or proactive aggression.

Flexibility in Teaching

No two children are the same. Each youngster views the world differently and has his or her own unique strengths and weaknesses. Therefore, it's important to individualize your teaching to tailor each child's needs.

Think of building a home. In every blueprint there are certain basic architectural guidelines that must be followed so that the house won't collapse in a storm or other natural events. However, you can change or modify various elements of the blueprint to fit your needs (e.g., larger kitchen, extra bedroom, two-car garage, and so on) without changing the strength of the structure. The structure of the Boys Town teaching methods works the same way; it provides caregivers with a solid blueprint or framework for teaching to aggressive youngsters, but leaves plenty of room for modification. These modifications may be necessary due to a number of factors,

Figure 1

Factors That Affect Teaching

Age of Child

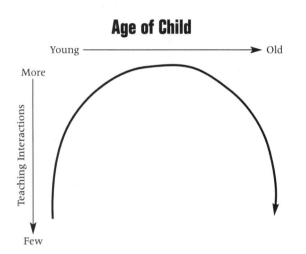

Skill Deficits

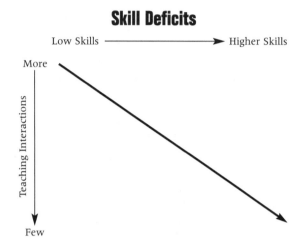

Length of Time in Program

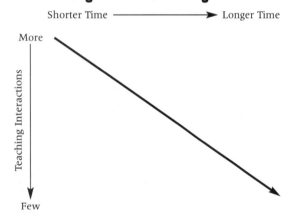

Developmental Stages

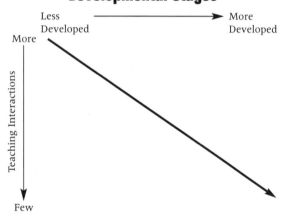

Ratio of Caregivers to Kids

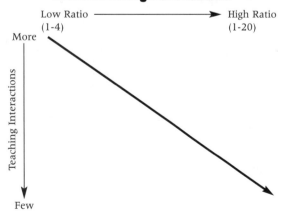

Relationships

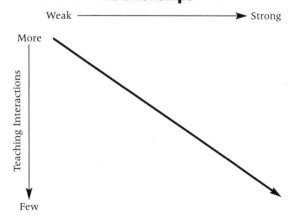

some of which are presented in Figure 1. (These factors mainly determine the frequency of teaching.) For teaching to be as effective as possible, caregivers must look at these factors and apply them to how they teach to each youth.

A youngster's age is the first factor to consider. Younger children respond better to teaching that is brief and specific. So, it's important to use language and examples in your teaching that are familiar and easy for the child to understand. The attention span of younger children is short, so don't belabor your teaching – get to the point as quickly as possible. In addition, you don't want to bombard younger children with lots of teaching. The younger a child is, the fewer times you will teach. As the child grows and matures, he or she will be better equipped to understand and handle more skills, and teaching can be done more frequently. Generally speaking, this all holds true for youngsters who have learning disabilities or mental or physical health problems.

As children get older and develop a solid foundation of skills, this pattern usually changes. They are more familiar with the behavior that is expected of them and the positive and negative consequences involved. So, the number of Teaching Interactions can decrease and they can be shorter.

The number of skills a child needs to learn is the second factor that will affect how and when teaching will occur. Children who have large skill deficits will require more teaching in order to help them learn new skills as quickly as possible. On the other hand, kids who have mastered a large number of skills will require fewer Teaching Interactions. This also applies to a child's developmental level. Youth who are more mature may require less teaching, while youngsters who are less mature may need more teaching.

For youth-care programs, there are two main factors that determine the amount of teaching that occurs – the length of time a youngster has been in the program and the ratio of staff to children. If a youth is new to a program, he or she will likely require more teaching. This is true because most kids who have been in a program for a short time have not yet learned, don't know how, or are not accustomed to using the basic skills that are necessary building blocks for learning more complex skills. Conversely, a child who has been in a program for a longer period of time has been taught certain skills numerous times, and knows what behaviors are expected.

When there is a lower caregiver-to-child ratio, caregivers will have more opportunities to teach. A caregiver who is responsible for four youngsters will have more time for teaching than a caregiver who is caring for 20 youth.

Finally, the relationships you develop with aggressive youngsters will have a great impact on the direction your teaching will take. At the beginning of a relationship and/or in a weak relationship, teaching will be more structured and take more time. But as your relationship with the youth grows stronger, less teaching should be required and your teaching will become more natural and brief.

Building Relationships

Attempting to help troubled youth change is difficult unless there is a strong relationship between a caregiver and a youth. Unfortunately, the importance of developing a relationship with children who have aggression problems is often undervalued, overlooked, and ignored by some adults. Instead, they try to control aggressive and violent children by demanding obedience and compliance, especially when these kids are upset or in crisis. This mentality only leads to disaster for both the caregiver and the child; a tug-of-war approach is what aggressive kids are used to and, more often than not, they will prevail. In reality, no one wins with this mindset. As a matter of fact, everyone loses. Caregivers and kids end up frustrated and angry with each other, and this ultimately has a devastating effect on the youngster's treatment.

When caregivers focus on building genuine, warm relationships with aggressive kids, they create a bond of trust, and kids begin to feel connected and worthwhile. They are much more likely to want to learn from and try to imitate a person who is warm, fun to be with, and dependable. In addition, caregivers can uncover and develop some of the redeeming and likable qualities that aggressive kids have in their personalities. Instead of continually wrestling to control youth, caregivers can begin to enjoy working with and being around the youth. As the relationship becomes stronger and matures, caregivers and youth start to have more good times together than bad. This can be a turning point for aggressive youngsters because they finally have the understanding and support they need to make the changes in their lives.

Teaching is what helps aggressive and violent kids learn new ways of thinking, feeling, and behaving. Teaching gives kids the skills they need to become responsible and independent people. But relationships make your teaching sincere and effective. By sending the message to children that you care about them, you give them a sense of belonging and self-worth. For many aggressive kids this may be the first time this has happened! Over time, these positive feelings become reciprocal; in other words, kids also start to care about and like you. When this happens, they are more receptive to your teaching and more willing to change for the better.

Building relationships comes naturally for some people; others may have to work at honing the skills and qualities necessary for creating a solid bond with troubled youngsters. But anyone who works with aggressive youth must make these skills and qualities part of their personalities and make using them a priority as they interact with and teach to kids. Caregivers cannot expect their teaching to make a lasting difference in a youth's life if there is no personal connection.

Here are some important skills and qualities that can help caregivers create and establish happy and healthy relationships with kids in their care:

◆ **Smiling** – This quality demonstrates warmth and can be used in many different situations. It's also free! Smiling makes people feel good inside. It comforts others when they are sad, lonely, or depressed. A simple smile can be an invitation to friendship, and a signal that a person is approachable and welcomes your presence. However, be careful not to smile at the wrong time, as aggressive youngsters might think you are laughing at them or making fun of them. For the most part, caregivers can't go wrong with a smile; it's an important ingredient to being viewed as open, easy to talk to, and friendly.

◆ **Having fun** – Many caregivers hesitate to have fun with the kids in their care for many reasons. Some caregivers are worried about losing authority and control, while others fear that showing a "human" side makes them vulnerable. Some caregivers rationalize that they are too busy dealing with other problems, while others simply don't know how to have fun. But having fun with kids is a great way to create an environment of warmth and acceptance while teaching kids valuable lessons about sharing, respecting others, taking responsibility, following rules, accepting defeat, or being gracious in defeat. There are many ways children can enjoy your company and your teaching without you losing any respect or authority (e.g., trivia quiz, a board or word game, playing catch or shooting baskets, and many others).

◆ **Humor** – Laughter is great medicine. Seeing or perceiving the amusing and funny events that happen every day and sharing a laugh with kids is extremely healthy both for the youth and for caregivers. Humor and laughter give kids a break from their daily struggle to overcome their aggression problems and from the other stresses in their lives. For caregivers, working with and caring for aggressive children is a tough job. Learning to find humor in what happens, especially during stressful times or crisis situations, can help insulate caregivers from the negative thoughts and feelings that can threaten to overwhelm them.

♦ **Learn to laugh at yourself** – All of us have shortcomings and we all make mistakes. Laughing at yourself means admitting that you have weaknesses just like everyone else. When caregivers are able to admit their mistakes and laugh at themselves, it sends the message to the kids that it's okay to make mistakes. But it is also important that caregivers model for kids how to learn from and correct mistakes and shortcomings.

♦ **Joking and teasing (appropriately)** – Telling funny jokes, joking with kids, and teasing in an appropriate way provides relief from the daily stress of life and allows caregivers and youth to better enjoy each other's company. However, joking and teasing can be a delicate area and caregivers must know what can and can't be said in certain situations with certain kids. Never joke or tease a child in a sarcastic or condescending manner; this will likely blow up in your face. Caregivers should take their time in this area and test the water. Some kids will understand the purpose and intent of your joking and teasing better than others and enjoy it; others, however, may interpret joking and teasing as a "put down" or a "slam." With these kids, caregivers should wait until they have developed a sound relationship before they begin joking and teasing.

♦ **Empathy** – Empathy means trying to understand another person's situation and feelings. When aggressive kids are in a treatment program, it is a very emotional and trying time in their lives. These kids are going through many tumultuous changes, and they often don't know how to handle the conflicting and confusing feelings and emotions that these changes bring. Empathy from caregivers can help kids through these rough times, and help them find the strength to carry on. Caregivers must accept the responsibility of providing a helping hand and an attentive ear to these kids. In order for troubled children to get better, they need to have a caring adult around who is willing to listen and acknowledge their feelings.

♦ **Praise** – Our society isn't very good in this area. Simply watch the nightly news or look at the front page of the newspaper; negativity and disaster abound. Only acts of unbelievable heroism or kindness are acknowledged, while almost all other good deeds go unnoticed. Adults have been conditioned to notice the negative things kids do; that means they often ignore the positive things kids do. Recognizing and praising kids' positive behavior might seem awkward at first because you aren't used to it, but praising kids is one of the most important tools in helping them get better. Caregivers must learn to focus on, recognize, and acknowledge kids when they do something right, no matter how small or insignificant it might seem. Kids thrive on your kind words and will likely repeat what they did in order to experience the good feelings that spring from your praise.

♦ **Listening** – Many troubled youngsters come from environments where parents or guardians live by the axiom, "Children should be seen and not heard." This may be one reason why some kids use aggression. In other words, many children and adolescents have learned to behave and act out aggressively to get the attention they crave. In their young minds, negative attention from adults is better than no attention at all. Kids need to have someone listen to what they have to say, especially when they are trying to change. Most of these kids haven't learned appropriate ways to communicate or express their feelings, so it's crucial for caregivers to listen carefully for cues that indicate what is bothering a youngster. By listening to children, caregivers can better understand the child and his or her individual problems, while demonstrating care, interest, and warmth.

◆ **Thoughtfulness** – This involves doing or saying nice things for someone else. Thoughtfulness is one of the biggest factors in developing relationships. It is extremely powerful and takes very little time or effort. Small things – a note or card, a phone call, a compliment, a smile or word of sympathy, remembering a birthday or special occasion – can mean a great deal to kids. These little acts of kindness add up over time. When troubled children see that you are sincere in your desire to help them get better, they begin to make you a welcome part of their lives.

◆ **Give and take** – Healthy relationships are not one-sided; there is an equal give and take. However, when you first begin working with and caring for aggressive youngsters, it will seem like you are doing all the giving and the youth is doing all the taking. Be patient! Not surprisingly, many troubled kids think only of themselves. For some time, they will be guarded and skeptical of your motives and intentions. But as the bond between you and youth grows, they will learn to reciprocate your warmth and concern. In order to overcome their aggression problem, kids have to learn to give their time, their compassion, and themselves.

Empowerment and Generalization

By teaching kids skills that help them to control their behavior, you are empowering youngsters to take control of their lives. When kids learn to use a skill in different situations on their own, they have "generalized" the skill. This means that a child who learned to use a skill in one situation knows how to use the skill in different situations without adult intervention. This also means that a social skill does not have to be retaught in every new setting or situation in order for a child to know how to use it. In the Boys Town Teaching Model, the belief is that if children have mastered social skills, they can use them anywhere.

Generalization can be promoted by having the youth thoroughly review and practice targeted skills under conditions that are as similar as possible to the real-life situations he or she may face. This way, they gain experience in dealing with real-life problems, issues, and events without having to worry about making mistakes or failing. This helps set them up for success in situations where they normally have problems.

With aggressive kids, the ultimate goal of the Boys Town approach is to help them overcome their problems by teaching new, appropriate ways for them to express and control their emotions and behaviors. As kids experience success with these new skills, they become confident in their ability to make the right choices. This improves their chances for success in society. Teaching social skills, building relationships, and empowering kids through teaching them self-control provides caregivers with a powerful approach to successfully managing and treating aggression in children and adolescents.

Measuring the Model's Effectiveness

Caring for and helping aggressive children and adolescents can be a difficult, discouraging, and, at times, unsafe task for caregivers. In many situations, these kids can be dangerous; in fact, many aggressive youth are capable of severely and permanently damaging their surroundings, or hurting others or themselves. Aggression is a problem that demands a model of care that has been proven to be effective and reliable. The Boys Town Teaching Model is such a model, combining modern, technology-based services along with genuine compassion and care to competently and successfully treat the needs of aggressive kids.

Proof of the Model's effectiveness comes from a recent study done by Friman et al. (1998). This ongoing study examined youngsters who were admitted to the residential program at Boys Town's Home Campus since

1993. Levels of aggression are measured at admission and then again 12 months later using the Diagnostic Interview Schedule for Children (DISC). The DISC, a structured interview for children and adolescents that allows mental health professionals to obtain diagnostic criteria information for common psychiatric disorders, is an important evaluation tool. It's widely used by mental health professionals in concert with the *Diagnostic and Statistical Manual of Mental Health Disorders (DSM-IV)*, the world's standard reference guide for evaluating and diagnosing mental health disorders in children, adolescents, and adults.

Friman et al. (1998) found that at admission, approximately 40 percent of the youth who were interviewed qualified for Conduct Disorder and 15 to 20 percent qualified for Oppositional Defiant Disorder. Children with these disorders exhibit a high amount of aggressive behavior, so treatment focuses on reducing aggression and teaching prosocial skills that can be used in place of aggressive behaviors.

When the level of aggression for youth in the study is measured with the DISC 12 months after admission, less than 5 percent qualify for either disorder. (See Figure 2.) Friman et al. (1998) concluded that the DISC results indicate that kids with aggression problems (within the context of Conduct Disorder or Oppositional Defiant Disorder) who are treated through the Boys Town Teaching Model for one year get dramatically better. In fact, there is an extremely strong likelihood that their aggression problems will be gone at the end of one year. The data obtained in this study is powerful support for the therapeutic effect that the Boys Town Teaching Model has on reducing aggression in children and adolescents.

Another way to address the question of effectiveness is to compare total scores from the Child Behavior Checklist (CBCL). The CBCL is one of the most commonly used tools in evaluating and measuring the effectiveness of a child's treatment. Administering the CBCL before the child enters a program and when he or she leaves the program provides

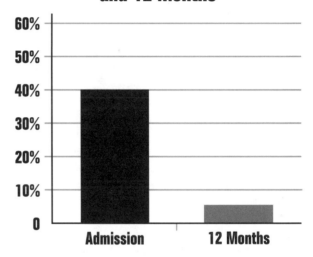

Figure 2

Main Campus: Percent of Children* with CD and/or ODD at Admission and 12 Months

*511 Boys Town residents were interviewed as part of this study

Adapted from Friman et al. (1998)

the scores for comparison. If the child's overall score on the CBCL is lower when he or she leaves than his or her score at arrival, it indicates that the child's behavioral/emotional problems have diminished and that treatment was effective.

Figure 3 (Thompson & Teare, 1997) shows this data across five Boys Town programs. (The CBCL data was acquired from records of all the youth served in these five programs during 1996.) In all five Boys Town programs, the total CBCL scores dropped dramatically from admission to departure, indicating that youth behavior/emotional problems – including aggression – diminished.

In addition, Boys Town specifically used the Aggression Score on the CBCL to measure the Model's effectiveness in reducing aggression in youth who received treatment at Boys Town's Intensive Residential Treatment Center (IRTC). The IRTC is the most restrictive level of care in Boys Town's System of Care; kids in this program require round-the-clock treatment for extremely severe mental health issues and problems – including very high levels of aggressive behavior.

The graph in Figure 4 shows the typical trends in the rate of aggressive incidents for two groups of youth who received treatment in the IRTC. (All the data are based on the information collected for the first 45 youth admitted to the IRTC in 1996.) The lower line (indicated by the solid squares) on the graph shows the typical trend of aggressive incidents for youth who scored average on their CBCL Aggression Score at admission. It's important to note that the mean CBCL Aggression Score of 75.3 is well into the clinical range, even though it is average for IRTC youth.

The upper line (indicated by the blank circles) on the graph shows the typical trend of aggressive incidents for youth who scored above average on their CBCL Aggression Score at admission. This means that these youth are even more aggressive than other IRTC youth. Both trend lines show a "honeymoon," or adjustment, period that lasts about one week, followed by a peak rate of aggressive incidents during a youth's second week in the program. After the second week, the rate of aggressive incidents for both groups of aggressive youth decreased for the next six months. This indicates that the behavior of aggressive youth who are admitted to and receive treatment in the Boys Town IRTC program improves.

Figure 3

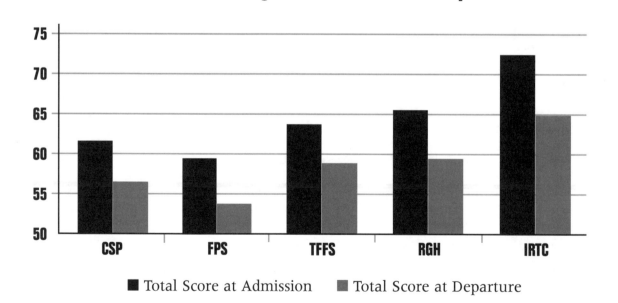

Is Care Effective?
CBCL Total Score Across Programs at Admission & Departure (1996)

■ Total Score at Admission   ■ Total Score at Departure

CSP - Common Sense Parenting
FPS - Family Preservation Services
TFFS - Treatment Foster Family Services
RGH - Residential Group Homes
IRTC - Intensive Residential Treatment Center

• A T-score is a standardized score where "normal" is considered at a score of 60 or below.
• Borderline Clinical Range: 60-63
• Clinical Range: 64+

Figure 4

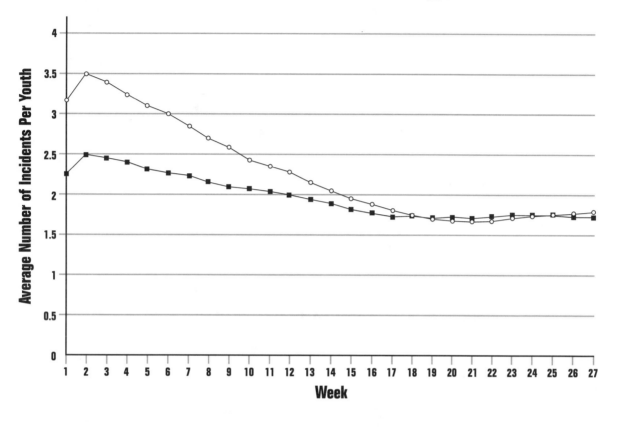

IRTC: CBCL Aggression Scores and Trends in Aggressive Incidents

—o— Above Average CBCL Aggression Score (85.3)

—■— Average CBCL Aggression Score (75.3)

Furthermore, the upper trend line shows that youth who were extremely aggressive prior to placement and initially have a higher rate of aggressive incidents get better faster than other IRTC youth. This pattern indicates that the Boys Town IRTC program is particularly effective in helping highly aggressive youth get better.

The final way to look at effectiveness is to examine the kind of environment youth go to once they leave a program. Figure 5 (Thompson & Teare, 1997) contains data that show that an overwhelming percentage of youth served in four Boys Town programs that were measured moved to a less-restrictive setting once they completed treatment. (This

data was obtained from records on all the youth served in the four programs during 1996.) This also is a very strong indicator that aggressive youth and youth with other behavioral/emotional problems get better during treatment in the various Boys Town programs that utilize the Boys Town Teaching Model.

Summary

The core of the Boys Town Teaching Model involves teaching social skills, building relationships, and empowering kids through self-control. The Model incorporates a social skill instruction approach – teaching youth positive alternative skills to replace negative behaviors – while also recognizing the importance and need for other types of treatment strategies, like medications and therapy, in successfully treating aggression in youth. Equally important to the success of a child's treatment is prescribing and assigning suitable social skills for targeted teaching by caregivers. Boys Town's extensive research has shown that social skill instruction is a valuable and effective treatment option in a wide variety of treatment settings for helping troubled youth overcome their aggression problem.

Boys Town's teaching methods have a structure that serves as a blueprint for care-givers when they teach to troubled and aggressive kids. But there also is flexibility built into this structure. The goal is to provide effective and therapeutic treatment for each and every child, and this is impossible to do with a rigid, blanket approach to teaching and treatment. In addition to these factors, building relationships with aggressive youth is imperative for teaching to be most effective. Finally, the Model empowers kids through teaching them self-control. This allows them to gain control over their emotions and behaviors so that they have a better chance of being successful in society.

Figure 5

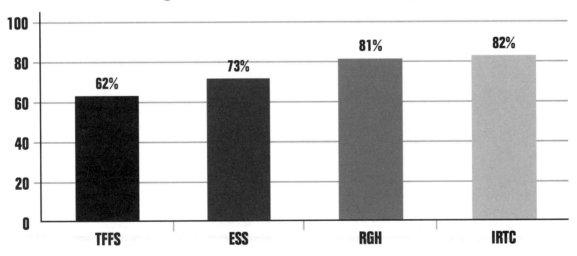

Is Care Effective?
Percent of Youth in Out-of-Home Placement
Discharged to a Less-Restrictive Setting (1996)

TFFS - Treatment Foster Family Services
ESS - Emergency Shelter Services
RGH - Residential Group Homes
IRTC - Intensive Residential Treatment Center

CHAPTER 4
Corrective Teaching

Kids constantly need teaching. Adults have many opportunities throughout each day to teach a youth something new, praise appropriate behavior, respond to a youth's failure to do what he or she should do, or correct a youngster's misbehavior. Teaching can involve anything from simple tasks like how to tie a shoe or set the dinner table to more difficult and complex issues like how to better control anger or solve a problem.

Kids are faced with new situations and dilemmas every day and they do their best to handle them. They deal with some problems better than others, but generally they need help and guidance from caregivers. Unfortunately, aggressive and violent kids tend to deal with their problems – both familiar and unfamiliar ones – in ways that produce negative and harmful consequences for themselves and those around them. These are the times when caregivers can step in and really make a difference in a youngster's life.

At Boys Town, Corrective Teaching (see Figure 1) is a process that caregivers use in response to a child's failure to do something he or she should do or to correct a youth's misbehavior. Obviously, this includes aggressive behavior. Through Corrective Teaching, caregivers teach alternative appropriate skills to replace the negative, aggressive behaviors that dominate a child's responses to the situations and people around him or her. Corrective Teaching also allows caregivers to share their experiences, knowledge, and abilities to help aggressive kids learn and grow socially and emotionally.

This proven teaching method consists of nine steps and is characterized by three central concepts – description, relationship, and consequence. Description includes specifically describing a behavior in words or actions, role-playing, and practice. The relationship concept involves using warmth and pleasantness, and showing genuine concern for the youth. It also involves helping the child to feel good about himself or herself. Consequences include feedback and losing a privilege for using an inappropriate behavior. For your teaching to be effective, there must be a balance among these three concepts.

The nine steps that make up Corrective Teaching provide the structure for this teaching

Figure 1

Corrective Teaching Components

1. **Initial praise/Empathy**

2. **Description/Demonstration of inappropriate behavior**

3. **Consequences**
   • Positive correction statement

4. **Description/Demonstration of appropriate behavior**

5. **Rationale**

6. **Request for acknowledgment**

7. **Practice**

8. **Feedback**
   • Positive consequence

9. **General praise**

method. However, as discussed in the previous section, many variables can affect how you use the steps, how many you use, and the order you will use them. Having structure ensures that the critical components are presented and helps make teaching consistent and effective. But if your teaching is to meet each youth's needs and fit the circumstances of the situation, you should be prepared to modify the teaching process. In this way, simple skills and complex skills can be taught to any child using the same basic method.

Let's take a closer look at the nine steps and their definitions:

1. Initial praise/Empathy – This is a way to begin teaching on a positive note. Using a statement of empathy (e.g., "I know this is hard for you.") lets kids know that someone cares enough to help. Praise statements (e.g., "Thanks for coming inside right away to talk with me.") recognize the child for using some positive behavior. Both of these statements are excellent ways to prevent a

youngster from reacting with volatile behaviors to your upcoming teaching and consequence.

2. Description/Demonstration of inappropriate behavior – Here you tell the child what he or she did wrong or failed to do. The description should be simple and brief so that the child can understand it. For some kids, especially younger children and youth at lower developmental levels, a demonstration may be necessary. A word of caution: Don't dwell on the description of the misbehavior. Caregivers can come across as "nagging" when they spend too much time re-hashing inappropriate behavior, and this can trigger a loss of self-control from youngsters.

3. Consequences – This step involves taking away something a youngster likes or giving something he or she doesn't like. For example, a caregiver might tell a youth that she can't use the phone the rest of the evening because she swore at and pushed another youngster. Or a caregiver might have a child do an extra chore for not following an instruction. (Boys Town uses Motivation Systems in which youth earn negative points for inappropriate behavior and positive points for appropriate behavior. Positive points can be exchanged for privileges. There also are other Motivation Systems, like sticker charts, that can be developed and used to meet the needs of each child and your type of program.) When giving consequences, it is important that children understand that their behavior earned the consequence and that they are responsible for that behavior. After the consequence is delivered, tell the child that he or she will have a chance to earn back part of the consequence (no more than half) for practicing an alternative appropriate skill with you. At Boys Town, this is called a positive correction statement, and it gives kids hope that all is not lost.

4. Description/Demonstration of appropriate behavior – In this step, you give a simple and brief explanation of the skill or behavior the youngster should use in place of the inappropriate behavior. Again, it is important to make sure your words or demonstration match the child's age and developmental level.

5. Rationale – This is an important step because it gives youth a reason for changing their behavior. In a sense, this is where caregivers "sell" the skill to kids. Generally speaking, younger children and kids who are new to teaching respond best to rationales that let them know the personal benefits of using the new behavior. A rationale that explains the negative consequences of continuing to use the old inappropriate behavior also works with these kids. With older kids and youngsters who are familiar with your teaching, caregivers should use "other-centered" rationales. These rationales let kids know how using a new skill or behavior will benefit others. Here, caregivers are helping kids move away from thinking only of themselves to thinking about how their behaviors and actions affect others. As a result, kids begin to learn and develop morals and positive values.

6. Request for acknowledgment – Simply put, caregivers ask youth if they understand the rationale and what is being taught. If the child doesn't understand the rationale, then caregivers should patiently give another one. It's important not to move on to the next step until the child lets you know that he or she understands what you are teaching. This is a step that can be used during teaching whenever a youth appears confused.

7. Practice – Here, the child is given an opportunity to use the new skill or behavior in a pretend situation. This gives the child a chance to be successful and gain confidence before he or she has to use the skill or behavior in a real-life situation.

8. Feedback – Following the practice, caregivers should tell the child how well he or she did using the new skill. This step gives caregivers the opportunity to help kids fine-tune their new behaviors. Depending on the situation, you may have the child do another practice or simply remind him or her to include anything that was left out the next time he or she has an opportunity to use the skill. After the practice and feedback, kids can earn back up to half of the consequence (positive correction). For example, if a youth lost telephone privileges for one hour as a consequence, he or she could earn back a maximum of 30 minutes of telephone time for practicing and accepting feedback. Positive correction serves as a powerful incentive for kids to take practicing seriously and not give up when the consequence is delivered.

9. General praise – This ends teaching on a positive note by recognizing and praising a youngster's efforts to learn and practice a new behavior. Praising kids at this time helps take their focus away from the consequence and allows them to leave the teaching session feeling good about themselves.

The longer a caregiver works with a youngster, the more natural teaching should become. Over time, a skillful caregiver will be able to determine exactly how to approach each Corrective Teaching opportunity and decide which steps are necessary for the child. By selectively using specific steps, a caregiver maintains structure in his or her teaching while continuing to interject personal qualities that strengthen the relationship. The result is a positive change in a youth's thoughts, feelings, and behaviors, and an overall change for the better.

Using the three concepts as guideposts and the nine steps as the "path" teaching should follow, let's look at two examples of how Corrective Teaching would look and sound with two different aggressive youth.

41

Example 1 – Bobby is a 10-year-old boy who is new to a caregiver's teaching. During free time, Bobby begins to argue with 8-year-old Tyrone about whose turn it is to choose a TV program. Bobby shouts and swears at Tyrone, and eventually pushes him down and changes the TV to the channel he wants to watch. Tyrone begins to cry and goes to tell the caregiver what happened. The caregiver calls Bobby upstairs, and they sit down at the kitchen table.

Caregiver: *"Bobby, thanks for coming upstairs right away.* (Initial praise) *Let's talk about what just happened downstairs. Swearing and pushing someone down in order to get something you want is wrong. You're bigger than Tyrone and could have hurt him."* (Description of the inappropriate behavior)

Bobby: *"But Tyrone was hogging the TV. It was my turn, and my favorite show was on."*

Caregiver: *"I understand that you really wanted to watch your program. But for swearing at Tyrone and pushing him down you've lost TV for one hour.* (Consequence) *Remember, you'll have a chance to earn some of that time back after we practice.* (Positive correction statement) *Okay?"*

Bobby: (nods his head in acknowledgment)

Caregiver: *"Super job of accepting your consequence, Bobby!* (Praise) *Now, let's talk about how to compromise with others. Next time you have a disagreement with someone, the best way to handle it is to remain calm. Then talk to the other person about what you would like to do and what he would like to do, and suggest something that both of you can agree on. If you aren't able to agree, stay calm, and go find an adult to help.* (Description of appropriate behavior) *That way, you're more likely to get what you want, and no one ends up getting hurt.* (Rationale) *Do you understand all that?"* (Request for acknowledgment)

Bobby: *"Yeah."*

Caregiver: *"Now let's practice how to compromise with others. Pretend that you're at home in the backyard and you want to use the swing that your sister is on. Do you remember the steps to compromising with others?"*

Bobby: *"Yes."*

Caregiver: *"Great. Let's practice what you are going to do and say. I'll pretend to be your sister and you are going to compromise with me about using the swing."*

Bobby: (looking at the caregiver) *"Jane, you've been on the swing for a long time. How about if we switch off and one person can swing for a while and the other person can play on the slide."* (Practice)

Caregiver: *"That was fantastic! You stayed calm and came up with an excellent option. Remember, if both of you aren't able to agree on a solution, continue to stay calm and go find your mom to help out.* (Feedback) *Since you did such a great job of practicing this new skill, you have earned back 20 minutes of TV time.* (Positive consequence) *Bobby, you did a super job of remaining calm this whole time and working hard with me on learning this new skill. I'm really proud of you!"* (General praise)

Now let's look at a similar scenario where a youngster has been exposed to a caregiver's Corrective Teaching for several months.

Example 2 – A caregiver is asking Beth, a 13-year-old girl, to apologize to Michelle for teasing her about her weight problem.

Caregiver: *"Beth, we need to talk for a minute. Michelle just told me you have been calling her names and teasing her about her weight."* (Description of inappropriate behavior)

Beth: *"But she's been such a pain. I'm sick and tired of listening to her talk about her weight all the time."*

Caregiver: *"I know it's hard to get along with everyone all the time* (Empathy), *but saying positive things to others is something you've been working on.* (Description of the appropriate behavior) *Remember, when you make positive comments about others you make them feel good about themselves, and Michelle needs that right now.* (Rationale) *We've gone over this before so you know that. For making negative comments to Michelle, you've earned an extra chore tonight –*

dusting and sweeping the basement. (Consequence) *Now I'd like you to go apologize to Michelle. Remember what to do?"*

Beth: *"Yes. I'll look at her, use a sincere voice, and tell her I'm sorry for calling her names and teasing her."*

Caregiver: *"Good. I appreciate you going over those steps.* (Praise and Feedback) *Michelle is in her room. She's still upset, so I'll go with you to see how things turn out."*

In the first example, the caregiver used every teaching step in order. This provided structure and ensured that the essential elements were included for a child who is just learning a new way to correct inappropriate behaviors. In the second situation, where the youth was familiar with the caregiver's teaching, the caregiver was able teach to the child in a brief, more natural style. In both cases, the caregivers dealt with the inappropriate behaviors with effective teaching and taught a skill. This illustrates the flexibility of Corrective Teaching, and how it can be modified as a child makes progress and becomes familiar with your expectations.

Summary

Kids will "mess up" and misbehave; in a sense, that's part of their job as youngsters. Caregivers must address these situations when they occur and view them as opportunities to help aggressive kids learn and grow. Corrective Teaching is one way to do this. It is a proven method for helping aggressive youth replace inappropriate behaviors with appropriate behaviors. The nine steps provide structure to the teaching process while enabling caregivers to develop and strengthen relationships with kids. What steps you use and how you use them is dependent on the child and his or her situation.

CHAPTER 5
Crisis Teaching

As you work with and care for aggressive youngsters, it is inevitable that they will sometimes become upset, angry, or frustrated. Even though you may be making progress in teaching new behaviors, many youth will fall back on their old aggressive behaviors in stressful situations. This amounts to a loss of self-control, which can make teaching difficult or impossible. But kids can learn to control their emotions and behaviors and, in turn, reduce their dependence on aggression. To teach the strategies kids need in order to achieve this goal, Boys Town uses a teaching technique called Crisis Teaching.

Crisis Teaching involves calming a child down so that a caregiver is able to teach self-control strategies. Simply put, self-control strategies are cognitive and behavioral techniques that empower kids to calm themselves when they become upset. (See Figure 1 for examples of self-control strategies.) They are easy to teach and can be used in a variety of settings. By using self-control strategies, youngsters are able to stop their usual negative responses, think of alternative ways of coping, and choose better ways of dealing with their problems. As kids learn to use these

calming techniques, they become more capable of getting their needs met in positive ways, and are better able to cope with stress, positively change their behaviors, and successfully resolve conflicts.

Eventually, kids learn to use these strategies on their own as they become more adept at recognizing and anticipating events that cause them to lose self-control and act out in negative and hostile ways. They learn the benefits that come from being able to manage their own behavior, control their impulses and feelings, live by rules and values, make decisions that are constructive rather than destructive, and deal with others in a more positive manner.

When kids are just starting to learn self-control strategies, caregivers spend a great deal of time teaching these strategies during "neutral" times. This means that there is no crisis, the child is not upset, and no negative behavior is occurring. The youngster is open and receptive to a caregiver's teaching, and teaching can be done with few distractions. By doing this, caregivers are better able to anticipate and head off problems and crises before

Figure 1

Examples of Self-Control Strategies

Deep-Breathing

♦ Take a deep breath in through your nose and hold it for about two seconds.

♦ Let the breath out slowly through your mouth.

♦ Repeat this process two or three times until you feel yourself calming down.

♦ When you are calm, tell an adult.

Journaling or Drawing

♦ Go to a designated place where you won't be disturbed.

♦ Write down (or draw a picture that shows) how you are feeling and what you are thinking.

♦ When you are calm, tell an adult.

Take Time to Cool Down

♦ Go to a designated place where you won't be disturbed or distracted.

♦ Take an agreed-on amount of time to calm down.

♦ If you need more time, calmly ask for it.

♦ When you are calm, tell an adult.

Positive Self-Talk

♦ Make a positive comment about how you can handle a situation appropriately. Use a phrase like, "I can get myself under control"; "I've done it before, I can do it again"; "If I stop now, things will get better"; or "I can do this."

♦ Repeat the statement you choose until you are calm.

♦ When you are calm, tell an adult.

Muscle Relaxation

♦ Clench and squeeze your fists for five seconds and slowly release them.

♦ Slowly roll your neck in circles for five seconds.

♦ Scrunch your shoulders and slowly roll them in circles several times.

♦ Slowly rotate your ankles.

♦ Raise your eyebrows as high as you can and slowly lower them.

♦ Scrunch your face and release.

♦ When you are calm, tell an adult.

they happen, while setting children up for success in situations where they previously made poor choices.

It is extremely important to choose the right self-control strategies for kids. They should meet each youth's individual needs, and be effective in times of crisis. To choose the best strategy for a child, keep in mind factors like a child's age and developmental level, the severity of a child's behaviors, how long a youngster has been exposed to your teaching, the different settings (e.g., school, sports, church, work, and so on) a child will be in, and a youth's willingness and desire to use specific self-control strategies as guidelines for matching strategies with the child's needs and abilities. (See pages 80-81 for a more detailed discussion of these factors.)

Typically, Crisis Teaching is used when inappropriate behavior continues to the point where it interferes with a caregiver's ability to teach. When this happens, the behaviors are referred to as **ongoing behaviors.** Ongoing behaviors can be subtle or overt, and range from passivity, withdrawal, silence, arguing, complaining, swearing, laughing, and not following instructions to making threats, damaging property, or physically assaulting another person.

No matter what ongoing behaviors occur, there is a common element that indicates the need for Crisis Teaching – the youngster is no longer following instructions. And regardless of the severity or intensity of the behaviors, this teaching method can be used to help the youth regain self-control.

Crisis Teaching consists of three phases which include a number of suggested steps. This provides the structure that is so important when teaching new behaviors to children. The three phases are:

♦ **Phase I – Staying Calm**

♦ **Phase II – De-escalating Behavior**

♦ **Phase III – Cognitive Strategies**

The following sections will provide an explanation of each phase and its steps.

Phase 1 – Staying Calm

There are two goals to the Staying Calm Phase. The first goal is to prevent extreme emotional outbursts – when possible. Realistically, some kids are going to have a crisis no matter how hard you work to prevent it. So, helping children quickly recognize and stop such outbursts when they do occur is the second goal in this phase. In other words, the youngster is given a chance to assess his or her negative behavior and stop it before it results in a full-blown crisis. The key to this phase is the caregiver's ability to shape and direct the child's behavior toward calming down.

It also is critical here for caregivers to remain calm and monitor their own behaviors. By remaining calm, caregivers model self-control, which may help the child to calm down. This also allows caregivers to focus on their teaching, and avoid using words or actions that may cause the child's behaviors to worsen.

Staying Calm Steps

♦ **Corrective Teaching begins (first consequence delivered).**

♦ **When ongoing behavior occurs, give the youth an instruction with a statement of empathy.**

♦ **If ongoing behavior continues, use the four ongoing tools:**

  1. **Give statements of understanding.**

  2. **Describe what was done wrong, and describe what to do right.**

  3. **Praise improvements in behavior.**

  4. **Give reality statements.**

(If you switch from one tool to another, pause and give the youth a chance to calm down.)

♦ **If ongoing behavior continues, deliver a second consequence for losing self-control. (This consequence is predetermined.)**

♦ **Offer the youth a chance to work through the problem. Include a positive correction statement.**

(If the youth agrees to calm down and begins to demonstrate self-control at this time, then return to the original issue. If the youth continues to engage in ongoing behavior, move to Phase II – De-escalating Behavior)

If the child continues his or her ongoing behavior, and will not discuss the situation calmly, begin Corrective Teaching. During this teaching, the child earns a consequence for the original inappropriate behavior. If the child continues the ongoing behavior, you can give a simple, firm instruction (e.g., "Right now you are swearing. A better choice is to stop talking."), or a statement of understanding to calm the youth (e.g., "I know it's hard to accept consequences all the time. Please sit down and stop swearing. I do want to listen to what you have to say."). If the child responds by following your instruction, you should generously praise him or her and decide whether it is necessary to continue the Crisis Teaching process. If the child is able to follow instructions and accept his or her consequences at this time, you should complete the Corrective Teaching Interaction.

(Note: If at any time during Phase I, the child regains self-control and stops the ongoing behaviors, it is not necessary to continue to the next step of Phase I. Complete your Corrective Teaching of the original issue and follow up on any positive correction statement you've made.)

If the child continues to engage in negative behaviors, there are four "tools" you can use to reduce it. The four tools are: statements of understanding (e.g., "I understand that you're angry right now."); describe what was done wrong and what to do right (e.g., "You're pointing a finger at me. Please put your arms to your side."); praise improvements in behavior (e.g., "You've stopped pacing. Nice job."); and give reality statements (e.g., "The sooner you start working with me, the sooner you can start doing some things you like doing."). When used skillfully by a caregiver, these four tools are extremely effective in helping an upset child regain self-control. Keep in mind that it is important to make use of the tool (or tools) that works best; that is, if one isn't working, try another. If you move from one tool to another, do so slowly, and continue to give the child a chance to calm down and remain calm.

The time you spend using the four tools will vary from child to child, and will depend on the intensity or severity of his or her behavior. If the child's inappropriate behavior increases in intensity and severity during this time, move to Phase II more quickly. But if the child responds in a positive manner to any of the four tools, continue to use the ones that are effective until the child calms down. If this happens, complete Corrective Teaching.

A word of caution is necessary here. As mentioned earlier, it is important during teaching to focus on the child's appropriate behavior as much as possible. Since one of the four tools calls for describing what the child is doing wrong, use this tool selectively. While it is important for the child to understand what he or she is doing wrong, frequently bringing up these behaviors can only serve to fuel the fire. The youth will view you as nagging, punishing, or belittling, and will be less likely to listen to what you are saying. Your goal should be to focus as much as possible on positive behaviors and to use praise whenever a child is displaying improvements in behavior. This takes a great deal of patience, skillful ability to observe and describe situations, and self-control.

If the child's inappropriate behaviors continue or escalate, the child may earn a second consequence; this one is for not maintaining self-control. When this happens, the consequence should be paired with a positive correction statement (e.g., "I understand that you're upset. Right now, you're not showing self-control and have earned a consequence. But you can earn some of the consequence back if you calm down and start working with me.").

The child's age and developmental level will determine how quickly you give this consequence. For younger children or those at a lower developmental level, you may give the consequence quickly because they have a shorter attention span and because the sole purpose of their behaviors many times is to get attention. With older children or those at a higher developmental level, you may give them a little longer to start regaining self-control. If the inappropriate behavior continues after a reasonable time, give the second consequence.

The final step in the Staying Calm Phase is to offer the child one last opportunity to work through the issue. You might say: "You can begin making good choices right now and work with me. Are you able to do this now?" If the child answers "Yes," you should tell the child how you expect him or her to listen and cooperate, then discuss the original issue and the child's loss of self-control. If the child responds appropriately, generously praise him or her for regaining control and return to teaching on the original issue. At this point, the child can earn back half of each of the two consequences; the first positive correction is for calmly discussing loss of self-control, and the second is for appropriately returning to the original issue. If the child does not respond appropriately, or continues to escalate an inappropriate behavior, it is time to move directly to the De-escalating Behavior Phase.

Phase II – De-escalating Behavior

Here, caregivers focus on helping the child choose and correctly use a self-control strategy that has been taught beforehand. As always, caregivers should remain calm and watch for improvements in the child's behaviors.

De-escalating Behavior Steps

♦ **Ask the youth to select a self-control strategy; if the youth cannot or will not, select one for him or her. If the child does select a strategy, he or she earns a positive consequence. (For examples of self-control strategies, see Figure 1.)**

♦ **Use the four ongoing tools and have the child use the self-control strategy. The four tools are: give statements of understanding; describe what was done wrong and describe what to do right; praise improvements in behavior; and give reality statements.**

♦ **Test the child's self-control with two simple instructions.**

♦ **Review with the child behaviors he or she should use that demonstrate self-control (e.g., calm voice, eye contact, sitting up straight, responding to questions, etc.).**

At the start of the De-escalating Behavior Phase, ask the child to choose a self-control strategy that he or she has learned (e.g., deep-breathing, muscle relaxation, journaling, positive self-talk, taking time to cool down).

If you have to choose a strategy for the child, he or she earns a negative consequence (which is given later in Phase III) for not choosing a self-control strategy on his or her own. If the child chooses a strategy, he or she earns a positive consequence, which also is given later in Phase III. The goal is to eventually empower the child to pick a self-control strategy on his or her own.

As we mentioned earlier, it is important to stay calm, talk in a nonthreatening voice, and talk slowly. Controlling your emotions is the single most important factor during this phase as you continue to offer statements of understanding and praise the child for any improvements in behavior as he or she begins to calm down (e.g., "Excellent, you stopped yelling. I know it's hard to stay calm when you're upset."). Positive correction statements let youngsters know that calming down and following instructions shows they are on the right path to regaining self-control.

Describing what the child is doing wrong and what he or she should be doing right also helps guide the child back to self-control (e.g., "You're walking around. Please sit down so we can talk."). When dealing with any ongoing inappropriate behavior, your instructions first should focus on the more overt behaviors, such as walking around, yelling, slamming doors, etc. (Again, use discretion here so that you don't continually repeat what the child is doing wrong.)

As this phase continues, the youth's behavior is likely to de-escalate and escalate several times. The goals are to reduce the number of times negative behavior escalates, decrease the length of time a child is in crisis, and increase the number of times the youth's behavior improves.

In addition to offering statements of understanding, describing correct behavior, and praising improvements, there are several other important factors to remember as you help the child resolve the situation. First, the youth may complain about the negative consequences he or she earns; you can respond with a statement of understanding and say that you are willing to help the child earn back some of the consequences (e.g., "I know you've lost something important. I'd like to help you earn back some of the consequence.").

During this phase, it is not necessary to continually talk to the youngster. If you respond to every comment the youth makes and try to fill in uncomfortable pauses or give too many instructions, he or she may view this as badgering. This may escalate the youth's inappropriate behavior. Insincere statements of praise or understanding also could further provoke the child. Use brief, easily understood statements and allow for appropriate pauses.

The youth may want to argue with you and set up a power struggle, or make demands (e.g., "I have the right to call my probation officer!"), accusations (e.g., "You're not fair to me!"), or statements aimed at making you angry. The child may act aggressively defiant in an attempt to get you to stop teaching and leave. Or, he or she may act passively defiant to make you upset. In all of these situations, the youth is trying to control your behavior. Don't be drawn into arguments or discussions of outside issues. Your primary task is to help the child regain self-control, and you must stay focused on that task. The best way to handle these types of behavior is to offer understanding statements and indicate a willingness to discuss an issue or consider a request after the youngster has calmed down. You then can redirect the youth back to the task at hand (e.g., "You can make that phone call after you calm down," or "I know you're upset and want to talk about fairness, but right now, please...."). By focusing on your teaching and varying the procedures to determine what works best, you can avoid getting sidetracked, which will only prolong the child's loss of self-control and disrupt the teaching process.

As you work through the crisis, stay reasonably close to the child. You should be close enough to talk, but not so close that you invade his or her private space; this could cause the child to strike out at you. In general, stay at least an arm's length away. If the youngster is walking around or leaves the room, stay nearby but don't "stalk" him or her by following too closely. If the youth is pacing around a room, simply stand in a strategic location or move a few feet one way or the other to stay reasonably close.

No matter whether the De-escalating Behavior Phase lasts several minutes or several hours or longer, the youth eventually will begin to make some progress toward calming down. Once you think the youth is ready to work with you, test whether he or she is calming down by giving simple instructions. Be careful not to give too many instructions (two should be enough) or instructions that could provoke more negative behavior. Before any teaching can be done, the youngster must be able to follow instructions – looking at you, acknowledging what you say, doing the task, and checking back.

Once the child is able to follow instructions appropriately and appears to have regained self-control, review and practice behaviors that demonstrate self-control. For example, you may tell the child that he or she should look at you, sit up straight, and respond to questions in a calm voice. These behaviors will demonstrate that the child has regained self-control and is now ready for teaching.

Phase III – Cognitive Strategies

Phase III begins when the youngster is calm and able to follow instructions, and is not using inappropriate behaviors. In the early steps of this phase, you should continue to praise and specifically describe any appropriate behavior.

Cognitive Strategies Steps

◆ **Prompt the youth on how to accept consequences (or practice).**

◆ **If the youth is calm and ready, review the consequences he or she earned. The consequences are:**

   1. **A negative consequence for not choosing a self-control strategy; a review and practice of the strategy is necessary.**

      OR

      A positive consequence for choosing a self-control strategy; no review and practice of the strategy is necessary.

   2. **A negative consequence for losing self-control.**

   3. **A negative consequence for the original inappropriate behavior.**

◆ **Give a positive correction consequence for the behaviors the youth is currently using that demonstrate self-control. This can be up to half of the negative consequence the youth earned for losing self-control.**

◆ **Return to the original issue and begin a Corrective Teaching Interaction with the step of describing the appropriate behavior.**

Because one goal of this phase is to get the youth to accept the consequences he or she has earned, remind the youth of the steps of that skill. If the youth does not appear completely ready to accept the consequences, you may choose to have him or her practice accepting consequences in a pretend situation. When the youth is ready, give the consequences. Praising the child for appropriate behaviors at this time is very critical (e.g., "You are really doing a super job of looking at me and nodding your head.").

(Note: If you had to select a self-control strategy for the youth, he or she earns a negative consequence. More teaching on making such choices, including a complete review and practice of a self-control strategy, is necessary. If the child picked a self-control strategy, he or she earns a positive consequence and no review or practice is necessary.)

Next, praise the child for remaining calm and following instructions during this phase. Specifically describe the behaviors the child is using that demonstrate self-control (e.g., remaining seated and quiet, looking at you, using a pleasant voice tone, and so on), and give the child a positive consequence for those behaviors.

The final step of this phase is to complete a Corrective Teaching Interaction on the original issue.

As you can see, there is an order and structure to the process of Crisis Teaching. However, this type of teaching also requires flexibility. Structure helps keep the teaching consistent and effective, and ensures that critical concepts are presented. Flexibility allows the person who is doing the teaching to modify the process to fit the child's needs and the circumstances of the situation. For example, you may have to use every step of Crisis Teaching with a child who is new to your program. On the other hand, you might shorten the process or use steps in a different order when teaching to a child who is familiar with your teaching style.

Remember, Crisis Teaching is not meant to be a rigid, all-or-nothing teaching tool. Structure is essential, but decisions on how to teach to children as individuals must be made based on your experience and ability, the children's needs, and the type of care you are providing.

Crisis Teaching Example

Let's take a look at how Crisis Teaching might sound the first time a caregiver addresses an aggressive youngster's loss of self-control. Keep in mind that Bill, the youth in this example, is new to the program, has no experience with Crisis Teaching, and is not familiar with the caregiver's teaching style. In this situation, the caregiver will provide more structure to his or her teaching by incorporating all the steps of Crisis Teaching.

Phase I — Staying Calm

Bill: *"Can I go outside and play some basketball?"*

Caregiver: *"Bill, thanks for asking permission so nicely. Right now we are getting ready for dinner, so this time I'll have to say 'No.'"*

Bill: (stands up and shouts) *"I'm sick and tired of this s----! You never let me do anything I want to do! You can't tell me what to do, you're not my parents!"*

Start Corrective Teaching

Caregiver: *"Bill, I understand it's hard for you to accept 'No' at times. Why don't you take a few deep breaths like we practiced so you can calm down."* (pause)

Bill: (begins to walk around the room and continues to yell) *"You are so d----- unfair, I can't believe it!"*

Caregiver: *"Bill, right now you are yelling and pacing around. For not accepting 'No' for an answer, you've earned a consequence. You will be able to earn some of that consequence back when we practice."*

Bill: (continuing to yell and pace) *"Shut up you a------!"* (pause)

Give a simple instruction with a statement of understanding

Caregiver: *"Bill, I know you're frustrated. But you're walking around the room and yelling. Please sit down in the chair."*

Bill: (angry voice tone and continued pacing) *"I can never do anything! I hate your f------ guts!"*

Ongoing behavior - use four tools

Give a statement of understanding

Caregiver: *"I understand you're upset and that you really want to play basketball."*

Bill: (shouting) *"You don't know a d--- thing about how I feel! Leave me alone!"*

Caregiver: (pause)

Describe what was done wrong and describe what to do right

Caregiver: *"Bill, right now you're shouting. A better choice is to lower your voice."*

Bill: (in a louder voice tone) *"This really s----! I hate it here!"*

Caregiver: (pause)

Praise improvements in behavior

Bill: (continues to walk around, but is no longer talking)

Caregiver: *"Thanks for quieting down, Bill."*

Bill: (yelling in angry voice tone and pointing a finger) *"Will you shut the f--- up! I'm not going to do anything you tell me, so leave me alone! All I want to do is go play some d--- basketball!"*

Caregiver: (pause)

Give a reality statement

Caregiver: *"Bill, the sooner you begin following instructions and calm down, the quicker you can start doing some things you like to do."*

Bill: (angrily yelling and pacing) *"I'm sick and tired of this s---! I can't believe how unfairly you treat me."*

Caregiver: (pause)

Give a statement of understanding

Caregiver: *"I know it's hard to follow instructions right now, but it is the only way we are going to get this problem solved."*

Bill: (still shouting and pacing) *"Are you deaf? I said I'm not going to follow any instructions!"*

Caregiver: (pause)

Bill: (yelling while moving closer to the caregiver) *"I ain't doin' nothin' and you can't make me!"*

Caregiver: (pause)

Bill: (stops a few feet from the caregiver with clenched fists, while also defiantly staring at the caregiver)

Give a second consequence

Caregiver: *"I know this is difficult for you, Bill, but for not showing self-control, you have earned an additional consequence.* (This consequence is predetermined.) *You can earn some of these consequences back if you calm down and work with me right now."*

Bill: (yelling and pacing) *"Go to h---! Your stupid consequences don't mean s--- to me."*

Caregiver: (pause)

Provide a final opportunity for the youth to work through the original issue; give a positive correction statement

Caregiver: *"Bill, you can begin making some good choices right now and begin working with me. Then you can earn back some of the consequences. Can you do that?"*

Bill: (yelling) *"Shut up and leave me alone, d--- it!"* (Bill picks up several magazines and forcefully throws them to the floor)

Phase II — De-escalating Behavior

Choose a self-control strategy

Caregiver: *"Bill, I know this is really tough for you and that you are angry. But you do have some choices. Can you choose a self-control strategy?"*

Bill: *"You bet I'm p----- off! You're always out to get me!"*

Caregiver: *"Deep-breathing is one of your self-control strategies. Why don't you take some deep breaths like we've practiced to calm yourself down."*

Bill: *"That crap is stupid! I'm not doing that."*

Use the four ongoing tools to help the youth regain self-control

Praise improvements in behavior

Bill: (stops pacing)

Caregiver: *"Great, Bill, you've stopped pacing. You're starting to make some good choices."*

Bill: (sits down and yells) *"I want to call my mom!"*

Caregiver: (pause)

Give a reality statement

Caregiver: *"Great job of staying in the chair. Once we work through this issue, we can talk about calling your mom."*

Bill: (yelling) *"I have the right to call my mom. I want to call her now!"*

Caregiver: (pause)

Describe what was done wrong and describe what to do right

Caregiver: *"I understand you have some concerns. Right now, you're yelling and a better choice is to stop talking and listen."*

Bill: (stops talking and remains sitting)

Caregiver: (pause)

Praise improvements in behavior

Caregiver: *"You've stopped talking; nice job of following instructions, Bill. You are starting to show some self-control."*

Bill: (remains in seat, quiet and angrily looking away)

Caregiver: (pause)

Statement of understanding

Caregiver: *"I know this is tough, Bill, and I know you're angry and upset."*

Note: Continue using the four tools until the youth engages in his or her self-control strategy and begins to calm down. Keep in mind that the length of the pauses will vary depending on the child's behavior. It is critical during this phase to provide the child with space so that he or she can stop the inappropriate behaviors. If a tool doesn't seem to be working or is causing the youth's behavior to escalate, stop using it and try another. Don't rush the process. Give ample time for the tools you are using to work.

Bill: (uses deep-breathing strategy and appears to calm down)

Test for self-control with simple instructions

Caregiver: *"Bill, you've done a nice job of getting yourself under control. You've done your deep-breathing, and you are remaining quiet and seated in the chair. I'm going to give you an instruction to check if you are ready to work through this problem."*

Bill: *"Okay."*

Caregiver: *"Thanks for using a pleasant voice tone. Great! I'm going to ask you to go pick up the magazines you threw on the floor. Remember to look at me, say 'Okay,' pick up the magazines, and ask, 'Is there anything else?'"*

Bill: (responds appropriately to the instruction)

Caregiver: (specifically describes and praises appropriate behavior; practices one more instruction with the youth)

Review behaviors that demonstrate self-control

Caregiver: *"You're doing a fantastic job of demonstrating self-control, Bill. Remember to keep using a calm voice tone, look at me, sit up straight, and give me an answer. Okay?"*

Bill: *"Okay."*

Phase III – Cognitive Strategies

(Keep in mind that the caregiver chose a self-control strategy for Bill.)

Prompt how to accept consequences (or practice)

Caregiver: *"Bill you've done a super job calming down. Keep it up. Do you remember how to accept consequences?"*

Bill: (calmly) *"Yeah."*

Review the consequences the youth earned

Caregiver: *"You have earned a consequence for not choosing a self-control strategy, for losing self-control, and for originally not accepting 'No' for an answer. But you can earn some of those consequences back when we practice."*

Bill: *"Okay."*

Caregiver: *"Great job of accepting those consequences!"*

Review and practice a self-control strategy

Caregiver: *"Okay, let's first look at what you can do the next time you get upset. Remember that when you want to use deep-breathing, or are asked to use it, you should take a deep breath in through your nose and hold it for about two seconds, let the breath out slowly through your mouth, and repeat this until you feel yourself calming down. When you are calm, tell an adult. Remember those steps?"*

Bill: *"Yeah. I just lost it."*

Caregiver: (asks Bill what other settings and situations he can use this self-control strategy in and why using a strategy is important)

Caregiver: *"Are you ready to practice this?"*

Bill: *"Okay."*

Caregiver: *"Remember, this is just a practice. I'm going to tell you that you can't watch TV. Remember what to do?"*

Bill: *"Yeah."* (Bill calmly asks to sit on the couch and does deep-breathing)

Caregiver: *"Great! You asked me if you could go sit on the couch, and you practiced how to use deep-breathing to calm yourself down. And you asked me in a quiet voice. Nice! It's important to remember to use one of your strategies the next time you get upset, no matter where you are or who you're with. Since you did such a good practice you have earned back half of the consequence you received for not choosing a self-control strategy."*

Child earns a positive consequence for using behaviors that demonstrate self-control

Caregiver: *"Bill, right now you are using a calm voice, sitting down, and really working well with me on practicing these skills. You are demonstrating self-control and have earned a positive consequence."*

Return to the original issue and begin a Corrective Teaching Interaction

Caregiver: *"Let's talk about the original issue of accepting 'No' for an answer. In the future, when you are given a 'No' answer you should...."* (The caregiver would finish a Corrective Teaching Interaction and the child could earn back up to half of the consequence for an acceptable practice.)

Making Good Teaching Better

When using Crisis Teaching, it is important to remember that your behavior directly affects the way a child behaves. Depending upon the severity of the child's behavior, you also may begin to feel upset, frustrated, or angry. These emotional responses can interfere with your ability to deal with the child's loss of self-control. If you become upset, it makes the child more upset and makes it more difficult to do constructive teaching. That's why it is essential that you remain as calm as possible.

It isn't always easy to stay calm when teaching. If a child is yelling, making threats, calling you or your loved ones names, or refusing to comply with instructions, you may initially respond emotionally rather than focusing on teaching to the youth's problem behaviors. If the goal of teaching during a crisis situation is for a child to learn self-control, it is essential for you to model self-control. The following information points out some of the important physical and emotional elements – what we call **quality components** – that must be present when you work with children who have lost self-control. These quality components also should be present when you are doing other kinds of teaching.

♦ **Offer youth "cool-down" time** – Kids can be given time to cool down whenever they are upset or frustrated, not just when they are in a crisis. Oftentimes, if a child has an opportunity to cool down right away, a crisis situation can be avoided. Otherwise, what starts as a small problem can become bigger and bigger, just like a snowball rolling down a hill. The child's ability to use a self-control strategy helps him or her stop negative thoughts, and gives the child something positive to work on.

♦ **Spend more time telling the child what he or she is doing right** – When a crisis occurs, adults tend to focus on what a child is doing wrong. It is easy to deal with these negative behaviors because they are visible, obvious, and sometimes "in your face." Focusing on a child's positive behaviors is difficult during a crisis situation. It doesn't seem natural. Positive behaviors are not as apparent, and your adrenaline is pumping, possibly causing you to become emotional. However, looking for positive

behaviors is a good way to divert your attention from the negative emotions you may be feeling. This can help you stay calm and give you something positive to say to the youth, which will help him or her calm down, too.

♦ **Talk softer and slower** – The tone and volume of your voice can have a big impact on how a child in crisis responds to you. Talking loudly or shouting can make a child think that you are yelling at him or her, while talking fast only confuses the youth. This is a bad combination and usually will escalate a crisis situation. As you concentrate on lowering your voice and talking slower, you begin to calm down. When you sound calm, you model how you want the child to speak. This is a big step toward averting or handling a crisis situation more quickly; such modeling can soften the intensity of a child's inappropriate behaviors and head off further escalation.

♦ **Remain physically relaxed** – Be aware of behaviors like clenching your fists, glaring at the child, pounding your hand on the table, towering over a kid, crossing your arms, and so on. A youth will perceive these kinds of actions as aggressive or threatening, and it will only make the situation worse. One excellent method for calming yourself physically is to take a deep breath, and let the air out slowly. Do this several times. This is an easy relaxation procedure that can be done quickly and almost anywhere. Your body will become less tense, and you will regain your composure.

♦ **Avoid arguing** – In a crisis, some kids are masters at dragging adults into arguments and debates about issues that have nothing to do with the problem at hand. Their goal is to move away from the issue so that you will forget about the difficulties they are having and the negative consequences they will earn. If you get caught up in these trivial arguments and debates, you'll not only lose, but also become more frustrated and angry. In these situations, you can keep your cool by letting the child know that you understand that he or she has some issues to discuss, and that you would be willing to discuss them once the child has calmed down and worked through the problem. Avoiding these debates is a good rule of thumb. But like any rule, there are exceptions. There will be times when immediately listening to what a child has to say can help solve a crisis. You will have to rely on your expertise and judgment to decide whether to discuss an issue during a crisis situation. There is no tried-and-true formula to tell you when it is right or wrong. The key is knowing the child you are working with and being sure that the behavior is one you don't normally see from that youth.

♦ **Watch your words** – Don't say things that "put down" kids. This only serves to escalate a crisis and ruin relationships. Be careful not to use a condescending or smug voice tone; how you speak also can send a negative message to the child. Another behavior that must be avoided at all times when teaching to kids is cursing or swearing. This is extremely unprofessional and poor modeling, and is a sure-fire way of intensifying a child's inappropriate behavior and badly damaging relationships. In addition, don't issue commands (e.g., "You need to sit down!"). These statements irritate kids and further escalate their behaviors. Instead, use "softer" words when making a request or giving a child an instruction; you can send the same message, but in a more gentle way. Making requests in a calm, cool, and collected manner increases the chances that a child will comply and successfully work through a crisis.

♦ **Use statements of empathy, understanding, and concern** – It is extremely hard for anyone to calm down – even adults – when they are angry or frustrated. Expecting kids to calm down quickly is unrealistic and demanding. Showing empathy and concern for an emotionally upset child helps defuse the highly charged emotions that can erupt during a crisis. It lets kids know that you understand what they are experiencing and are concerned about their well-being.

♦ **Use positive correction** – Some time during your teaching, you will give a negative consequence for a child's behavior. This usually involves taking away all or part of a privilege or something else the child likes. Many times when this happens, kids don't see any light at the end of the tunnel and focus solely on what they just lost. That's why it's important to tell kids they will have a chance to earn back some of the consequence by practicing behaviors you want to see. Positive correction statements give kids a ray of hope. It may be just what they need to hear in order to begin to calm down.

♦ **Know your child** – Every child has unique needs, and this will be reflected in the way you teach. Many variables must be considered when implementing the steps of Crisis Teaching. As we said earlier, this process is not rigid, but a natural series of behaviors and responses to those behaviors. Its success relies on your ability to know your child, and to determine which components to use, and when and how to use them.

Calming kids down and teaching self-control strategies during Crisis Teaching is an interactive process. If you aren't careful, some kids may try to manipulate you and "teach" you to use inappropriate behaviors. It is important to always be aware of your own behaviors, especially during times when you may become upset. If you can't control yourself, it is impossible to teach a child how to maintain self-control. When you remain calm, kids have the time they need to calm down and think about the self-control strategies they want to use. The goal should not be to control children, but to teach them how to exercise self-control.

Summary

Teaching aggressive kids various individual, effective, and therapeutic strategies for maintaining self-control is one of the most important treatment objectives of the Boys Town Teaching Model. These children and adolescents experience many unpleasant feelings (e.g., sadness, anger, jealousy, and so on) due to traumatic events in their lives. These overwhelming feelings often are expressed in aggressive, violent, and self-destructive behaviors when a crisis occurs.

There are three phases to Crisis Teaching and each phase has its own steps. However, it's important to remember that each child's needs and situation is unique, so be flexible during a crisis and use what works. Self-control strategies are what help troubled kids deal with unpleasant feelings, anticipate crisis events, and calm themselves instead of exploding with combative, antagonistic, and damaging behaviors. In this way, youth learn different methods to successfully manage crisis situations and get their needs met in a more socially appropriate manner.

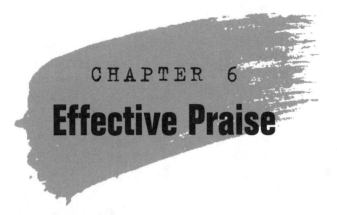

CHAPTER 6

Effective Praise

Kids make mistakes – that's to be expected. It comes with the territory of being a young person. But for every mistake or misdeed, there are many, many things that a youngster says or does that are positive and should be praised and reinforced. With some children, caregivers have to look much longer and harder to find these positive qualities, skills, and behaviors. When working with and caring for aggressive and violent youngsters, this is often one of the most challenging tasks for caregivers.

In today's society, adults have a tendency to expect kids to behave appropriately and make the right choices. But when kids do, they rarely receive praise and encouragement. And without praise and encouragement, a child sees no reason to continue to do good things; his or her positive skills and behaviors are not reinforced and likely won't occur again. In the Boys Town Teaching Model, "catching kids being good" and reinforcing them with praise when they do something right, correctly use a skill, or engage in a prosocial behavior – no matter how small or insignificant it might seem – is a critical component to helping aggressive kids get better.

It isn't always easy for kids to "do the right thing." Many factors – friends, television, music, and others – can influence or encourage youth to take a dangerous or destructive path. That is why caregivers must be able to recognize and praise positive behavior and accomplishments when they occur. At Boys Town, Effective Praise is the teaching method that caregivers use to identify and reinforce positive qualities, skills, behaviors, and accomplishments so that kids will repeat them and, ultimately, make them a permanent part of their lives.

As a matter of fact, praising kids' prosocial behaviors is so important to effective teaching that Boys Town recommends that caregivers recognize or praise 4 to 10 or more positive behaviors for every one negative behavior a child displays. This means, for example, that caregivers should recognize and praise at least four positive behaviors for every Corrective Teaching Interaction they do with kids. This ratio is based on the needs and circumstances of each child. For instance, kids who are younger, new to your teaching, or have severe treatment issues will likely require a higher positive-to-negative ratio than kids who are older, familiar with your teaching, or have less-severe problems.

As you can see, Effective Praise should be your most frequently used Teaching Interaction. That's because people – especially kids – thrive on the attention of other human beings. Kids need words of approval, pats on the back, smiles, and recognition of their accomplishments in order to become happy, healthy individuals.

This chapter will focus on how to use Effective Praise to bring about changes in aggressive youth.

Factors that Make Praise Powerful

Praise can be one of the most powerful teaching methods you use. But it also can be misused and ineffective if you aren't aware of some important principles. Here are four principles that must be incorporated into a caregiver's Effective Praise Interaction to make praise powerful, effective, and therapeutic:

♦ **Immediate** – Praise works best when it is given immediately after the desired behavior or skill occurs. This means that the connection between the praise and the positive behavior that is being praised is clearer and stronger. This, in turn, makes it more likely that the child will use the behavior again because he or she wants to be praised. For example, a caregiver observes a child ignoring some teasing from other kids. In order to effectively reinforce and strengthen the positive behavior of ignoring the teasing of others, the caregiver praises the youngster immediately. If the caregiver waits until the end of the day or the next day to praise the youth for his positive behavior, the praise either will not be as powerful or won't have the desired effect.

♦ **Contingent** – Caregivers should provide praise (i.e., positive reinforcement) only when the desired behavior or skill is

displayed by the youngster. Keep in mind that a behavior is strengthened when it is immediately followed by praise or some other type of positive reinforcer (e.g., pat on the back, tangible reward, etc.). Thus, the behavior must occur before a reinforcer is given. In this way, the praise or reinforcer is directly linked to the youngster's accomplishment.

♦ **Specific** – Caregivers should be as specific as possible when describing positive behavior or accomplishments to a youngster. This helps the youth understand exactly what he or she said or did, making it easier for the child to duplicate the appropriate behavior again in the future. Using only vague statements like "Nice job" or "That was great" can leave a child confused about what he or she did that was so nice or great. In fact, there is a danger that another, less desirable behavior may be accidentally reinforced when the reason for the praise isn't clear.

♦ **Credible** – Praise is only effective if it is personal, sincere, and focused on improvement. If a caregiver praises kids all the time without any apparent purpose, the youth will become confused and not believe that a caregiver's praise is sincere. Therefore, praise is no longer effective in bringing about change. For example, a swimming instructor constantly and indiscriminately tells his pupils, "Great job" and "Way to go." When a mother asks her daughter how she is progressing in swim lessons, the girl replies, "I don't know." The mother, confused, says, "But I just heard your instructor tell you that you were doing a great job." "Yeah," the young girl says. "But he tells everyone that, even the kids who can't swim." Praise loses its "clout" when it is used for everything a child does. Be selective and make praise count. Also, make sure your facial expression, voice tone, and mannerisms match your praise. A dour look and a bland, monotone voice are not very reinforcing and won't lend credence to your words.

The Effective Praise Interaction

Effective Praise is crucial to developing healthy relationships with kids, and is very important in developing and strengthening appropriate behavior. This teaching technique allows caregivers to sincerely and enthusiastically recognize the progress each youngster is making. Like Corrective Teaching and Crisis Teaching, there is a structure to Effective Praise. And the same factors that affect other types of teaching also affect how you use these steps. (See "Factors That Affect Teaching" on page 30.)

Effective Praise Components

1. **Initial praise and skill identification**

2. **Description/Demonstration of appropriate behavior**

3. **Rationale**

4. **Request for acknowledgment**

5. **Positive consequence**

6. **General praise**

Let's take a closer look at the six steps and their definitions.

1. Initial praise and skill identification – Caregivers should begin each interaction on a positive, upbeat, and enthusiastic note by praising youth for their appropriate behavior. Be sure to identify the skill that is related to the behavior you are praising. Hearing the name of the skill will help many youth, especially younger children and youth at lower developmental levels, gain a clearer understanding of what you are praising and what they should continue to do.

2. Description/Demonstration of appropriate behavior – Here, caregivers should specifically describe, or demonstrate if necessary, a child's verbal and nonverbal behavior. In other words,

tell the child exactly what he or she did right and what he or she should continue to do in the future. Keep in mind that it is important to use words or a demonstration that matches the child's age and developmental level.

3. Rationale – A rationale is a reason given by caregivers that explains to children why it's important to use a skill and helps them "buy into" the behavior. In Effective Praise, caregivers will focus on two types of rationales: how using the skill benefits the youth (personal-benefit rationales) and how using the skill benefits others (other-centered rationales). (Avoid using rationales in which children are told they should use a certain skill only to avoid negative consequences.) Caregivers should shift from using personal-benefit rationales to other-centered rationales as soon as it is appropriate for each youth.

4. Request for acknowledgment – As discussed earlier, this is the step where caregivers ask youth if they understand the rationale. Remember, if the child doesn't understand the rationale, give another one, and don't proceed to the next step until you feel that the youth understands.

5. Positive consequence – Here, the child earns a positive consequence as a reward for his or her appropriate behavior. This increases the likelihood that the behavior or skill will be used in similar situations. The positive consequence should be something the youth likes or wants; what reinforces one child may not reinforce another child. Positive consequences can range from social reinforcers like verbal praise, pats on the back, and smiles, to tangible reinforcers like extra time on the phone, a pop with dinner, or going to a movie. It's important to keep in mind that the positive consequence should be large enough to keep the child interested in continuing to use the desired behavior. For example, a positive consequence of two extra minutes for playing games on the computer may not be large enough to motivate a child to use a behavior again. However, 10 or 15 minutes of extra time might better capture the child's attention. Over time, the size and type of consequences you use should be faded away so that kids don't rely on external rewards. For instance, during the time it takes for a child to master a given skill, a caregiver should gradually switch from giving tangible types of rewards when the child is just beginning to learn the skill, to social kinds of rewards like pats on the back or verbal praise as the youth gets better at using the skill. Eventually, a simple non-verbal signal like a "thumbs-up" or a smile will be a sufficient consequence for recognizing the child's mastery of the desired skill or behavior. The goal here is to help youngsters eventually internalize a positive behavior and use it because it's the right thing to do, not because they'll get something they like or want.

6. General praise – Caregivers should end the interaction with a sincere, enthusiastic statement of praise or appreciation for the youth's efforts and encourage the child to keep working on his or her positive behaviors.

Now, let's take a look at two examples of how Effective Praise would work with two different kids.

Example 1 – Julie is an 11-year-old girl who is new to the caregiver's teaching; one of her primary treatment goals is reducing incidents of aggressive behavior. In this scenario, the caregiver asked Julie to begin her homework. This time, Julie responded appropriately. In the past, Julie refused to follow this instruction, and the caregiver used Corrective Teaching and even Crisis Teaching.

Caregiver: *"Julie, that was great! Just a second ago, you did a fantastic job of following instructions."* (Initial praise and skill identification)

Julie: (smiling) *"Thanks."*

Caregiver: *"When I asked you to get your books and begin study hour, you looked at me and said, 'Okay, I'll get on it.' Then, you went upstairs, got your books, and told me you were ready to go. That's a great job of following instructions.* (Description of appropriate behavior) *When you follow instructions right away, you're more likely to finish your homework and other tasks quicker. That way you'll have more free time to do some things you like to do, like riding your bike.* (Rationale) *Does that make sense?"* (Request for acknowledgment)

Julie: *"Yeah, it does."*

Caregiver: *"Since you did such a super job of following instructions, you've earned an extra 15 minutes outside after study time. That way you'll be able to ride your bike a little longer.'* (Positive consequence)

Julie: (smiling) *"All right!"*

Caregiver: *"Julie, you've been trying real hard lately. Keep up the good work!"* (General praise)

Example 2 – Jeff is a 15-year-old boy who has been living with a caregiver for three months. The first couple of weeks, Jeff had problems accepting "No" for an answer. Since then, Jeff has consistently responded appropriately to "No" answers. In this example, Jeff asked to go to a movie and his caregiver told him he couldn't because the movie was not appropriate for his age. Jeff responded appropriately by saying, "Okay."

Caregiver: *"Jeff, nice job of accepting 'No' when I said you couldn't go to the movie.* (Initial praise and identification of the skill) Caregiver pats Jeff on the back. (Positive consequence) *Remember that if you can accept 'No' answers without arguing, you have a better chance of getting a 'Yes' answer in the future, if possible.* (Rationale) *Now, let's look for a different movie."*

Summary

Learning and using a new skill or behavior is difficult for kids and involves many behavioral steps. That is why caregivers must take great care to recognize, validate, and reward even the smallest signs of progress. Praising these accomplishments encourages kids to keep trying, and lets them know that their efforts are worthwhile. In order for aggressive children and adolescents to get better, they need recognition and appreciation. The more ways and times a caregiver can find to praise youngsters for their efforts to learn, the faster they will learn. Effective Praise allows caregivers to sincerely and enthusiastically recognize the progress that each youth is making, while enhancing each youth's confidence and feelings of competence.

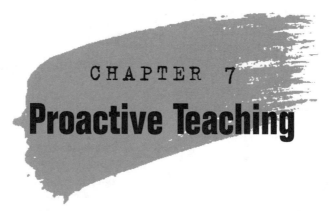

CHAPTER 7
Proactive Teaching

When aggressive kids are just starting to learn new social skills to replace problem behaviors, caregivers will spend a great deal of time doing what we call Proactive Teaching. Proactive Teaching is used to teach new skills before a youth will need to use them and to anticipate and head off problems and crises before they happen. When you prepare youth for problems before they occur, kids are set up for success in situations where they previously made poor choices. As a child starts using these newly learned skills and begins experiencing success, you will be viewed as helpful and concerned, which helps to further develop and enhance positive relationships. Proactive Teaching can be a real key to a youth's success and your sense of accomplishment.

Proactive Teaching can be used to teach youth basic and advanced social skills, prepare youth for specific situations or circumstances, and address specific skill deficiencies. This type of teaching can be done individually or with a group of youth, depending on the circumstances.

There are many opportunities for this type of preventive teaching during the course of a day. As youth make progress and begin to use their new skills and behaviors, you can spend less time doing Proactive Teaching and rely more on cues and verbal prompts instead. Eventually, kids will consistently and correctly use these skills as they begin to successfully resolve problems and conflicts on their own. Achieving this goal isn't always easy; in fact it often can be slow, arduous, and frustrating. Caregivers must remain patient and continue to make the most of their opportunities to teach proactively if they are to help aggressive youngsters learn new ways to control their behavior.

It's important to use Proactive Teaching during "neutral times." These are times when the youth is calm and not misbehaving, and is not involved in an activity, and the environment is relatively free from distractions. This makes it easier for the youngster to remain attentive and focused during the teaching sessions, and makes the child more receptive to your teaching.

Caregivers should keep these teaching sessions as short as possible, while maintaining high quality. Proactive Teaching opportunities generally occur at times when kids could be doing something they like to do, so if caregivers spend a lot of time teaching, kids get bored and "antsy." If this happens, teaching actually can become counter-productive and it can sabotage future sessions because the youngster views this time as a nuisance. In addition, it is essential to keep the teaching session upbeat, positive, and interactive. Kids learn better when the teaching atmosphere is fun, and when they are active participants instead of passive observers.

Proactive Teaching has eight steps; caregivers should use all eight in every session. This is necessary because each step has an important function in teaching children new social skills and/or preparing them for new situations.

Proactive Teaching Components

1. **Introduce skill/Give examples**

2. **Describe/Demonstrate skill components**

3. **Rationale**

4. **Request acknowledgment**

5. **Practice cue**

6. **Practice feedback**
   • Praise and describe performance

7. **Positive consequence**

8. **Prompt future practice/Praise**

Let's take a closer look at the eight steps and their definitions.

1. Introduce skill/Give examples – Caregivers should tell the youngster what they will be discussing and identify the specific skill area that will be taught. Next, caregivers should give examples of the settings (e.g., home, school, sports team, work, etc.) where the skill can be used so that kids understand that the skill is important to their success in many different environments.

2. Describe/Demonstrate skill components – Here, caregivers should break the skill down into specific, understandable steps. If necessary, caregivers can provide a demonstration to ensure that the youngster knows the steps and how to use them.

3. Rationale – As in the other Teaching Interactions, caregivers provide a reason for why it's important to use the new skill or behavior. Keep in mind that rationales should be brief and to the point, not long-winded explanations or lectures. One way to make Proactive Teaching more interactive is to ask the youth why he or she thinks it's important to use the skill.

4. Request acknowledgment – Caregivers ask the child if he or she understands the rationale. This component also helps get the youth involved in the teaching session and can be used all throughout the interaction.

5. Practice cue – In this step, caregivers should have the youth practice the skill immediately so he or she can become comfortable with the component behaviors. This also allows caregivers to assess their teaching. A role-play or pretend situation that is appropriate to the age and developmental level of the child can be used to give the youth a realistic opportunity to practice the new skill. When the practice is set up, caregivers should carefully explain what will happen and review the skill components again. To make teaching even more effective, practice sessions should be as fun and reinforcing as possible.

6. Practice feedback – Since the skill is new to the youngster, it is unlikely that he or she will initially get all the steps right. Caregivers should encourage the youngster by praising behaviors that are performed correctly, and nonjudgmentally describe those that need improvement. If the youth is having difficulty with some components, caregivers should make sure that the steps are not too difficult and have been explained clearly, and that the skill is age-appropriate. The youth can practice the skill again, as long as this step doesn't become too lengthy.

7. Positive consequence – It is critical that kids earn positive consequences for practicing and learning a new skill. Caregivers must remember that this teaching is usually done when youth could be doing other things they like to do. So caregivers should provide a positive consequence to help ensure that kids will want to participate in Proactive Teaching again.

8. Prompt future practice/Praise – Caregivers should let kids know that they will be practicing this, and other skills, in the future. One technique caregivers can use is to follow up this initial Proactive Teaching session with other quick role-plays throughout the day. After each role-play, caregivers should provide descriptive praise, a description of the appropriate behaviors, and a positive consequence. This will help the youth learn the skill as quickly as possible. Finally, caregivers should praise the child for his or her participation and effort during the teaching session.

Now, let's see what a Proactive Teaching example might sound like.

Example – Carla is a 13-year-old girl who is receiving help for her aggression problem. Being new, Carla needs help learning some of the basic social skills that can be used to replace her aggressive behaviors. One skill she needs to begin working on is *"Accepting Criticism."*

Caregiver: *"Carla, let's take a few minutes to talk about a new skill called 'Accepting Criticism.'*

It's not always easy to do, but it will help you be successful here, and at home and school. It will even help when you're playing volleyball for your school. I know that volleyball is really important to you! Does your coach ever give you feedback and tell you to do things differently?" (Introduce skill/Give examples)

Carla: (laughing) *"Yeah, she's always telling us to change something or to hustle and stuff like that."*

Caregiver: (smiling) *"When I played sports, my coaches were like that too! So, when you're given criticism by someone – your mom, or teacher, or volleyball coach – you should look at the person, say 'Okay,' and don't argue.* (Describe skill components) *That way people like your volleyball coach will be more likely to want to help you, and you'll have a better shot at making the team and getting playing time.* (Rationale) *Make sense?"* (Request acknowledgment)

Carla: "Yes."

Caregiver: *"Great! Now let's practice accepting criticism. Let's say I'm your volleyball coach and I'm going to give you feedback on your serve. Remember to look at me and say 'Okay' without arguing. Got it?"* (Practice cue)

Carla: *"Sure, I got it."*

(Caregiver gives pretend criticism and Carla responds appropriately.)

Caregiver: *"Outstanding, Carla! After I gave you that criticism, you looked at me, said 'All right, coach,' and didn't argue at all. That's the way to accept criticism!* (Practice feedback) *Because you did such a nice job here, you've earned an extra snack after dinner.* (Positive consequence) *Super job! Now, later today I'm going to come to you and give you some criticism. It may be pretend or real, so be prepared to use the steps we just went over, okay?"* (Prompt future practice/Praise)

Summary

Proactive Teaching is a valuable teaching tool for both caregivers and kids. This teaching technique helps caregivers prepare youth for unfamiliar situations and promotes gradual behavior changes in areas where youth have previously had problems. When youngsters learn how to change their behaviors and handle problems, they feel good about themselves and their confidence in their abilities soars! Proactive Teaching allows caregivers and aggressive kids to work toward goals together, which strengthens relationships. Taking time to set kids up for success through Proactive Teaching is one of the most valuable teaching methods a caregiver has at his or her disposal in helping children and adolescents overcome their aggression problem.

CHAPTER 8
Preparing to Do Treatment Plans

Aggressive youngsters come to you with varied histories and assorted problems, and they require help for different reasons. But the treatment goal for every aggressive child is essentially the same: To reduce and, when possible, eliminate aggressive behavior so the child can become a productive and valued member of his or her family and society. Unfortunately, there is no "magical cure" for every child's aggression problem. Helping aggressive kids is a complex and demanding goal for caregivers because each child is unique and requires individual treatment. That is why being prepared for the treatment planning process is the single most important task for caregivers as they try to help aggressive kids get better.

In the first two parts of this book, we've laid a foundation to help prepare you for developing effective and therapeutic Treatment Plans for aggressive kids. So far, we've discussed what aggression is and what it is not, how to distinguish between proactive and reactive aggression, and the important role that the Boys Town Teaching Model and its specific teaching methods can play in treating aggression. But there's still a little bit

more to know before you begin choosing and using strategies for treatment. Specifically, this includes an explanation of some principles of behavior and a look at a unique evaluation approach that helps you determine why a youth uses aggression. This information will allow you to become better at selecting appropriate strategies for each child's Treatment Plan.

Successful treatment planning begins with an in-depth, thorough, and careful evaluation process. Beginning the journey to reduce aggression is pointless unless caregivers know what has happened in a youngster's life and understand why he or she uses aggressive behavior. Neglecting this information is like a doctor trying to treat patients without knowing what is wrong with them. The doctor may get lucky and occasionally prescribe the right remedy, but more often than not he or she will miss the mark and the patient will not get better. In many instances, the patient's condition will worsen because the doctor prescribed the wrong medicine or treatment. Simply put, an inadequate evaluation frequently leads to a misdiagnosis, which results in ineffective and even harmful treatment.

A good doctor is trained to complete a comprehensive evaluation that requires a thorough examination, tests, and questions about a person's ailment and medical history. The doctor takes his or her time during this assessment process because it is essential for an accurate diagnosis, which ultimately leads to responsible treatment. Skilled caregivers must use the same care and consideration in their evaluation of aggressive youth. Caregivers and others involved in a child's treatment must complete a thorough assessment so they can choose the best strategies. Once caregivers discover the scope and depth of a child's aggression problem, then and only then can they confidently begin constructing an effective and therapeutic Treatment Plan.

This chapter contains a discussion of some principles of behavior that are important for caregivers to be familiar with. In addition, we will present an evaluation process that can help you uncover the reasons kids use aggressive behavior. In Chapters 9 and 10, we will offer some specific ideas and strategies for developing effective, workable Treatment Plans for kids who tend to use proactive or reactive aggression. Those two chapters also will include samples of Treatment Plans that can be used in different programs and treatment settings.

Principles of Behavior and Assessing Aggression

Caregivers can't simply provide custodial care or just be passive observers or "baby-sitters" for troubled youth and expect results. In the Boys Town Model, caregivers are active participants, teaching social skills and developing close and caring relationships with kids. Teaching social skills is an important treatment strategy and a big part of a Treatment Plan because it enables caregivers to be direct agents of change and to guide and adjust a youth's treatment.

In order to competently assess a youngster's problem and confidently choose and assign appropriate skill sets for a Treatment Plan, caregivers must have a fundamental knowledge of some basic principles of behavior. These principles make up some of the "science" behind the Boys Town Teaching Model. The Model applies these basic principles of behavior so that children can learn to choose for themselves a course of action that is most beneficial to them and others.

Behavioral principles are the fundamental laws or assumptions concerning the nature of behavior. They attempt to define and explain the relationships between a behavior and the specific conditions surrounding the behavior. In other words, these principles are statements of the natural causes and effects of behavior.

In order to understand how to assess and identify the "payoff" – or reasons – for aggressive behavior in children and adolescents, it is necessary to become acquainted with the terms and definitions of some principles of behavior. These are discussed in the following sections.

The ABC Pattern

Sam is a 14-year-old boy who has been in an out-of-home treatment program for about four weeks primarily due to physical aggression toward others. One day after study hour, Sam and the other kids were asked to go to their rooms and put away their school books. As they walked down the hall, one boy dropped his homework folder and all his papers scattered over the hallway floor. Sam and most of the other kids had not gotten along with this younger boy since he arrived four days earlier. Laughing loudly, Sam called the boy a "clumsy a------." The other youngsters in the hallway laughed at Sam's comment, patted him on the back, and said, "Way to go! You finally shut up that little s---." The younger boy began to cry, got up, and ran down the hallway to "go tell on" Sam.

——— ◆ ———

Behavior does not occur in a vacuum. Events that happen in the environment or are present before and after a behavior can have a major impact on that behavior. For example, in the situation with Sam, seeing the boy drop his homework papers (what happened before) prompted Sam to call the younger boy a name (Sam's behavior). The other kids in the hallway laughed at Sam's negative comment (what happened after). The attention from the other kids was Sam's "payoff" for his aggressive behavior. It is important to understand what happens before and after a behavior so that the behavior itself can be fully understood. This enables caregivers to choose the most effective treatment strategies and, in the case of social skill instruction, the best social skills to target for teaching.

The terms used to identify these events make up the ABC pattern:

A = Antecedents – the events or conditions present before a behavior occurs.

B = Behavior – anything a person says or does that can be observed and measured.

C = Consequences – the events or conditions that occur after a behavior.

Antecedents

The events or conditions that are present before a behavior occurs can range from simple to complex. For example, a telephone ringing is a simple antecedent to the behavior of answering the phone. In this case, a single event (the phone ringing) occurred prior to someone answering the phone. However, other complex antecedent conditions that affect the behavior of answering the phone could be present. A person who has a history of receiving bad news on the phone may feel anxious, begin thinking about who it could be and what bad news the call might bring, and hesitate before answering. A person in the middle of a heated argument might answer the phone with a harsh voice tone or not answer the phone at all. A person who is high on drugs might hear the phone ring but not answer it because it would interrupt the drug experience.

When analyzing the antecedents of a behavior, it is important to pay particular attention to what you can observe: the who, what, when, and where of the situation. In other words, who was present, what activities were occurring, when did the behavior occur (the time of day or day of week, season of the year, and so on), and the location or physical setting. Other important antecedent conditions, which are more difficult to observe can include a person's history of reinforcement, thoughts, emotional arousal, or other physiological influences such as illness or drugs. These events or conditions may combine in different ways to become antecedents of behavior.

Behavior

Behavior is anything a person says or does that can be observed and measured. It can be observed directly or indirectly. For example, caregivers can directly observe a youth sweeping the floor, cursing, or apologizing. (Concepts such as intelligence, anger, or depression are not behaviors; they are labels for sets of behaviors that people often group together for ease of reference.)

Indirectly observing behaviors involves observing the results of behavior. If someone swept the floor, you could see a clean floor; if someone hit another person, you could see bruises or scars; if someone injected drugs, you could see marks on a person's skin. In addition, physiological "behaviors" that happen "inside" a person can not be directly observed, but some can be measured with special equipment.

Consequences

Events or conditions that follow a behavior are known as consequences. Consequences can be pleasant, unpleasant, or neutral. In terms of the teaching methods we've discussed, consequences can involve something that is given or added or something that is taken away. A pleasant event that

71

occurs following a behavior and the removal of an unpleasant event after a behavior are both likely to increase the use of that behavior. Receiving an "A" on a test (pleasant event) as a result of studying hard should motivate a student to study hard in the future. Hitting the "snooze" button to turn off the alarm clock in the morning (removal of an unpleasant event) may result in an increased use of the snooze button.

A behavior tends to decrease if an unpleasant event occurs, or if a pleasant event is taken away, following the behavior. For example, calling a friend and getting cussed out (an unpleasant event) may decrease your behavior of calling that friend. Having to pay a fine for speeding (money – something pleasant – is taken away) can result in less speeding.

Knowing the events and conditions that occur following a behavior can help you analyze why the behavior is occurring, determine whether it is likely to increase or decrease (or stay the same), and plan effective treatment strategies.

Understanding Aggressive Behavior: A Three-Dimensional Approach

Generally, children (and adults) tend to repeat behaviors that in the past have resulted in pleasant events for them or the removal or avoidance of unpleasant events. For example, an aggressive child may tease and belittle others in school because it draws the attention of his classmates (like Sam in the earlier example). Another child may engage in noncompliance, yelling, threatening, cursing, and hitting in order to get out of having to go to school.

Understanding the reasons for human behavior is so challenging because behavior is so complex. It's clear that a wide range of antecedents and consequences can influence behavior. For example, a child may regularly use certain physically aggressive behaviors like hitting and fighting only under certain antecedent conditions, perhaps when peers tease or shun him. Under other antecedent circumstances, the same child may use different aggressive behaviors to get out of doing an unpleasant task. Since such aggression has helped him avoid tasks in the past, he uses the same aggressive behaviors whenever he's told to do a chore.

In analyzing the difficult behaviors that make up aggression, it may be helpful to use a three-dimensional approach. (See Figure 1.) According to Stumphauzer (1986), this involves breaking antecedents, behaviors, and consequences (dimension one) into specific categories (dimension two), while also recognizing that each category has a complete history of reinforcement (dimension three). We've already discussed the ABC's of behavior that make up dimension one. Here is a description of the categories that make up the second dimension:

♦ **Situational** – the influence of the situation (other than social influences)

♦ **Social** – the influence of other people in the environment

♦ **Cognitive** – the influence of thoughts

♦ **Emotional** – the influence of emotions or states of arousal

♦ **Other physiological** – physiological influences other than those that are emotional

It is important to stress that the total of all these events and conditions contribute to making up an antecedent, behavior, or consequence. Categorizing the ABC's of a behavior is an arbitrary process and simply is a way to help one understand the reasons for certain behavior.

While this categorization is helpful, it is not complete without the child's history of reinforcement. The reinforcement history represents the third dimension to understanding

Figure 1

The Three-Dimensional Approach

	Antecedents	Behavior	Consequences
Situational			
Social			
Emotional			
Cognitive			
Physiological			

History of Reinforcement

the function of behavior. Each category included in the second dimension has a complete history of being reinforced, not reinforced, or punished under certain circumstances. This reinforcement history influences whether or not a behavior occurs.

Let's look at how this three-dimensional approach applies to an example of an older boy who uses physically aggressive behaviors (e.g., hitting and fighting) to get a younger child's radio. (See Figure 2, adapted from Stumphauzer, 1986.)

As you can see, the various influences on antecedents, behavior, and consequences, coupled with a person's learning history, can result in a complex matrix of behavior. But there is yet another analysis to be completed. That involves looking at the payoff for each

category of behavior. In the example of an older youth hitting a younger child to get a radio, here are some possible payoffs or functions:

♦ **Situational** – The older youth easily obtains the radio he wants and does not get caught. This may increase the likelihood that such behavior will occur in the future.

♦ **Socially** – Lots of reinforcement from peers in the form of praise, approval, and admiration may increase the likelihood that such behavior will occur in the future.

♦ **Emotionally** – The emotions felt by the older youth (initially anger, followed by a general increased arousal) may be reinforced by the success of obtaining the radio, and increase the likelihood that the same behavior will occur in the future.

Figure 2

Example of Payoff for Physical Aggression

	Antecedents	Behavior	Consequences
Situational	Younger, smaller child, no adults present	Punched younger child to get radio	Now have a new radio
Social	Peers suggest, support hitting other youth	Peers continue to support	Now have a new radio
Emotional	Aroused due to anger over not having a radio	Heightened arousal and excitement	Excited, relieved, arousal decreasing
Cognitive	"I'm strong and smart, I won't get caught"	"You can do it, no adult is around"	"I did it, this is great, my friends are impressed"
Physiological	Inhibitions reduced by alcohol	Alcohol effects: reduced reaction time, etc.	Continued effects of alcohol

History of Reinforcement

◆ **Cognitively** – Thoughts of being strong, dominating others, being too smart to get caught, and peer approval are being reinforced and will likely lead to a repeat of the behavior in the future under similar circumstances.

◆ **Other physiological** – Using alcohol or drugs may have reinforced all of the above events, and the positive effects or sensations that come with being drunk or "high" may outweigh the long-term negative physical and emotional effects of drinking or using drugs (e.g., hangover, fatigue, depression, etc.).

Given this hypothetical situation, do you think the older youth will continue to use physical aggression in order to get what he wants under similar antecedent conditions in the future? Because the behaviors of hitting and fighting are being reinforced at all these levels in this situation, there's a good chance that this youth will hit and fight again.

Summary

When planning treatment for children who engage in any aggressive behavior (e.g., noncompliance, yelling, cursing, verbal threats, stealing, harming animals, punching, fighting, and so on), it is extremely helpful to look at antecedents, behavior, and consequences, how these are directly influenced by the various categories, and the history of reinforcement for each category. Using this three-dimensional approach to gain an understanding of the "payoff" of aggressive behavior for children helps caregivers to choose the best treatment strategies.

In addition to this assessment process, there are several other sources of information at caregivers' disposal that can help provide valuable insight into understanding why a child uses aggressive behavior. Some of these include psychological reports, social histories, and other admission reports; parent or guardian interviews and reports; youth interviews; caregiver observations; and others. The point here is that caregivers should gather as much information as possible during the evaluation process so that they are able to determine why a child is using aggression. Once caregivers collect all this information and identify the reasons for a youth's aggressive behavior, they are better prepared to develop therapeutic, effective Treatment Plans.

CHAPTER 9
Treatment Strategies for Reactive Aggression

Planning and providing treatment for aggressive children is an awesome responsibility and a tough job for caregivers. When caregivers are able to evaluate and identify the reasons or motivation for aggressive behavior, they can better determine whether the behavior is proactive or reactive. Once a child's aggression problem is classified, a caregiver can select strategies that are designed to tackle specific inappropriate behaviors and integrate those strategies into a Treatment Plan.

Reactive aggressive kids tend to be bothered and upset by the actions and reactions of others. They are impulsive and respond to what happens around them in an emotionally charged manner. When they become upset, reactive aggressive youth have great difficulty controlling their aggressive behaviors. Typically, they use their aggressive behavior to avoid and/or escape problems that stem from their contact or relationships with others. This aggression regularly harms and, many times, severely damages these relationships. That's why one focus of treatment planning for reactive aggressive youth should be teaching new skills that enable kids to solve their problems in ways that are socially acceptable and not harmful to relationships.

The following sections discuss and explain some treatment strategies that Boys Town has found helpful and effective in treating reactive aggression in children and adolescents. It's important to keep in mind that using only one of these interventions in a Treatment Plan is not likely to bring about the desired changes in a troubled youth's aggressive behavior. Instead, selecting and implementing a combination of strategies helps to make a Treatment Plan therapeutic and successful. The last section of the chapter includes two case studies and sample Treatment Plans from two different treatment settings. These are presented to demonstrate this multidimensional approach to treating aggression.

Social Skill Instruction

As we have stressed throughout this book, social skill instruction should play a major role in the treatment of any aggressive youth. An integral component of the Boys Town Teaching Model, this treatment strategy has

77

been proven to dramatically reduce both proactive and reactive aggression in children. Treatment Plans for kids with these behavior problems are much more likely to succeed when they focus on teaching skills that foster self-control and the ability to make positive behavioral choices.

Several factors can enhance the use of social skill instruction when caregivers are helping reactive aggressive youth. Those factors are discussed here.

Accentuate the Positive

Many reactive aggressive youth have unhealthy and hurtful relationships with others. Because these kids have directed unpredictable and impulsive acts of aggression toward others, those "victims" have reacted negatively toward the youth or developed a negative perception of them. As a result, many reactive aggressive kids are not well-liked and have experienced much criticism. When these kids come to you for treatment, they are extremely wary and distrustful of others; many times they don't seem to want help. That is why Effective Praise is such an important Teaching Interaction for caregivers.

Caregivers should try to "catch" reactive aggressive kids using positive behaviors as often as possible. Boys Town recommends that you praise kids much more often than you correct them during treatment. Depending on the child's problems and his or her situation, a positive-to-negative ratio of 10:1 or higher can be appropriate and therapeutic. (You may recall that this means trying to do 10 Effective Praise Interactions with a youth to recognize appropriate behavior for every one Corrective or Crisis Teaching Interaction.)

Because many aggressive kids have such severe relationship problems, it's vital that caregivers establish a strong, healthy bond with each youth as soon as possible. Effective Praise can help accomplish this goal. Over time, as caregivers point out and reinforce the good things youth do – often some of these

may seem small or insignificant – kids begin to feel good about themselves. As they come to realize that the caregivers' praise is genuine, the confidence kids have in themselves and their ability to overcome aggression problems soars.

Catching kids being good through lots of Effective Praise helps build trust with kids; they begin to believe you really want to help them get better. Eventually, the walls these kids have put up around themselves crumble, and they start to work with you instead of against you. When kids allow you to enter their lives, you have a much better chance of helping them overcome problems.

Set Kids Up for Success

Life is full of new people and experiences; not all of them are good or pleasant. A large part of succeeding in life depends on how well a person learns to deal with difficult and unpleasant circumstances. When people have the opportunity to plan and rehearse for these upcoming difficult events, they are much more likely to succeed than if they go in cold and unprepared.

Unfortunately, reactive aggressive kids have learned to respond in harmful and destructive ways when they face new experiences that cause upset and turmoil. Oftentimes, they don't think about the consequences of their aggressive behavior – they just erupt. So an important treatment goal for many reactive aggressive youth is to learn how to "look before they leap." In other words, caregivers should teach kids to stop before they act and to think of the best appropriate way to handle a given situation.

Incorporating extra Proactive Teaching sessions into a Treatment Plan is a strategy that can help achieve this goal. Caregivers can set kids up for success by preparing them to properly respond to situations that have caused problems in the past or new situations that will likely lead to an aggressive response. For example, if a child is about to have a meeting with the school principal, helping her practice conversation skills that she can use in place of aggressive behaviors will likely lead to a successful outcome. A youth who has a history of becoming aggressive when other kids tease him should practice skills for appropriately dealing with teasing before his first day of school. When youngsters are given the opportunity to rehearse prosocial skills and proper responses before difficult situations, they are much more likely to succeed and learn how to react in similar situations.

One way to make Proactive Teaching even more powerful is to use what we call a *preventive prompt*: Just before a difficult event or situation, a youth is given a prompt or reminder of what he or she practiced in a Proactive Teaching session. For instance, just before a child meets with the principal or walks into the school for a new school year, you give a quick reminder to use the appropriate skills and responses that were practiced earlier.

Another type of preventive treatment strategy involves helping kids recognize physiological signs (e.g., quick breathing, fast heartbeat, flushed face, racing thoughts, tingling in hands, etc.) that precede aggressive responses. Youth then learn to respond to these signs by using a self-control strategy.

Proactive Teaching, preventive prompts, and recognizing physiological cues that precede aggression are extremely effective with reactive aggressive children and adolescents because each strategy acts as a stop sign, signaling youth to pause and think about how to appropriately handle a difficult situation. As children learn to better recognize and handle difficult situations on their own, caregivers won't have to use prompts and Proactive Teaching as often. When kids experience success where they once experienced only failure, they will view you as concerned and helpful. This helps to further develop and enhance positive relationships.

Don't Fuel the Fire

Reactive aggressive kids are especially likely to react with extreme outbursts in Corrective Teaching and Crisis Teaching situations. Why? One reason is that youngsters resist consequences that they don't like or think are unfair. While consequences are a necessary component of effective teaching, how caregivers give them often determines how a child will react.

To avert a negative reaction when doing Corrective Teaching with a reactive aggressive youth, make sure to follow up a consequence with a positive correction statement. In other words, tell the child that he or she has an opportunity to earn back some of the consequence for practicing the appropriate alternative skill. Remember, positive correction lets kids know that all is not lost; it helps soften the blow of a negative consequence and helps prevent a negative outburst.

Crisis Teaching is a very delicate time. A crisis is looming, but a caregiver often can skillfully manage its severity and duration simply by giving the child opportunities to use a self-control strategy to calm down. Also, avoid giving a barrage of consequences by moving slowly and carefully through each step of Crisis Teaching. Remember, the goal here is to get the child to stop his or her aggressive behavior and choose and correctly use a self-control strategy. Quickly delivering consequences and racing through the interaction doesn't give the reactive aggressive child enough time to process what he or she should do. In fact, it almost guarantees that the child will revert to his or her old, familiar aggressive behaviors instead of trying to use new, appropriate skills. Moving too quickly also can perpetuate and even escalate a crisis.

Self-Control Strategies

As you might recall, self-control strategies are behavioral and cognitive techniques that empower kids to calm themselves down. Generally, these strategies are used during crisis situations and other times when there is upset and turmoil in a child's life. The goal when teaching youngsters self-control strategies is to enable them to recognize the need for, choose, and correctly use a calming strategy like deep-breathing or positive self-talk (see Figure 1 on page 46 for other examples of self-control strategies) on their own before they erupt in aggressive and violent ways.

Two Teaching Interactions that are especially useful in helping youth learn self-control strategies are Effective Praise and Proactive Teaching.

Since it will be difficult for youth who have been so locked into aggressive responses to change their behavior and use new strategies, progress often will be slow. Youth will face many setbacks and sometimes they may feel like they're not getting anywhere. That's why it is important that caregivers use Effective Praise to reinforce a youth's efforts to make even the smallest improvements in his or her behavior. Youth who see that you are behind them, providing support and guidance because you genuinely want them to get better, are more likely to stick with the treatment program, even when times are tough. Getting youth to commit to and believe in the goals they are trying to achieve is a major accomplishment, and Effective Praise can help you get there.

Frequent Proactive Teaching sessions also should be incorporated into a youth's Treatment Plan. These teaching sessions are most effective when they occur during "neutral times," when the child is neither upset nor displaying negative behavior, and there are few or no distractions in the environment. When using Proactive Teaching, caregivers should set up role-plays that are realistic and as close as possible to the issues and situations that have caused the youth to lose self-control in the past. For example, if a child who is new to your teaching consistently becomes upset and begins to yell, curse, and throw things when she is told she can't do something she wants to do, it is important to review and practice the new skill of *Accepting "No" Answers,* and review and practice how to choose and correctly use a self-control strategy. (This is especially critical when kids are first learning a skill or are having difficulty using a particular skill.) In this type of situation, there may be many instances when Crisis Teaching and self-control strategies are needed. However, as the child becomes more proficient at accepting "No" answers, Crisis Teaching and the use of self-control strategies will be required less frequently.

Choosing Individual Self-Control Strategies for a Treatment Plan

It is extremely important to choose the right self-control strategies for kids who are not able to appropriately express or deal with anger, frustration, conflict, and crisis. These strategies should meet a youth's individual needs, and work best for that youth in times of crisis. As you consider the strategies presented in Chapter 5, these factors should serve as guidelines for matching techniques with the needs of each child.

◆ **Age and developmental level** – Some self-control strategies are geared for and are more suited to older youth, while other strategies are more appropriate for younger children. For example, drawing would be a better strategy than writing in a journal for a younger child who has not yet learned to write or a youth who is unable to express himself or herself through writing. In these cases, choosing the wrong strategies can actually lead to a crisis situation because the child becomes frustrated by his or her inability to perform them. Strategies like drawing, deep-breathing, and taking time to calm down that divert the child's attention away from the crisis situation are most effective with younger or developmentally handicapped children.

♦ **Severity of behaviors** – Many troubled youth have behavior problems that are quite severe. Problems that jeopardize the safety of the child or others may initially call for self-control strategies that are appropriate for a situation, simple to teach, and easy for the youth to use anywhere. For example, if a boy who has a history of being physically aggressive toward others is facing a crisis situation, giving him a pen to write in a journal with could create an extremely dangerous situation. Instead, calming techniques like deep-breathing, muscle relaxation, or positive self-talk would work better and be safer.

♦ **Exposure to teaching** – The length of time you have been working with a youth on self-control issues also will play a role in determining appropriate strategies. A child who has been participating in treatment for some time and has been making progress in using calming techniques may be ready to learn more advanced strategies. With these kids, calming strategies such as writing in a journal, progressive muscle relaxation, positive self-talk, anger logs, hassle logs, and others may be extremely effective and therapeutic. On the other hand, children who are new to your teaching would concentrate more on basic calming techniques.

As a youth gets better at using self-control strategies, you can begin to teach new ones. For example, a child may progress from going to his bedroom to draw in a notebook when he gets upset at home, to writing in a journal at the kitchen table, to using deep-breathing in any situation where he experiences frustration or anger. This process usually develops and improves slowly over time, so be patient. The longer a child is exposed to your teaching and has opportunities to practice and use a self-control strategy, the better he or she will get at choosing to use the strategy on his or her own.

♦ **Setting** – Some settings are more suitable for specific self-control strategies than others. For example, a child can use the strategy of drawing in his room at home. However, this may not be an appropriate strategy to use outside the home. That's why it is important for children to learn a number of self-control strategies that can be used in different settings (e.g., school, sports, church, work, and so on).

♦ **Child's response** – This factor involves a child's willingness to learn and use a particular self-control strategy, and its observed effectiveness. It is fruitless to try to teach a strategy that a youth does not want to use. In addition, if you observe that a child is not using a certain calming technique, then it may be necessary to replace it with a different strategy. One of the best ways to prevent this from happening is to have the child help choose which strategies will be taught and used. This gives the child a sense of ownership and involvement, and makes it more likely that he or she will use these strategies in crisis situations.

Keep in mind that the five self-control strategies listed in Chapter 5 are examples of calming techniques that Boys Town has effectively used to help aggressive kids. This is by no means an all-inclusive list of self-control strategies. With some kids, caregivers may have to create and develop effective calming techniques. The point here is that it's very important for caregivers to teach strategies that work best for each youth.

Distorted Thinking

One factor that can cause a child to react aggressively is distorted thinking. This means that the youth is either inaccurately perceiving cues from others or is misreading their intent. In order for children to change their reactive aggressive behaviors, they must learn how to recognize their distortions and how to change their thinking so they can assess situations more accurately and more positively.

Before discussing how to help children in this area, it is important to understand some of the common cognitive distortions that play a role in reactive aggressive behavior. Here is a list of some of these distortions:

♦ **Filtering** – This occurs when a youth dwells exclusively on a single negative detail of a situation, ignoring all the positive aspects. Consider this example: Jack writes a paper for English class. The teacher returns it with the remarks, "Well written, Jack. Good subject matter and keeps the reader interested. Next time, provide more detail about your subject." When Jack reads this, he ignores the teacher's positive comments and concentrates only on her suggestion to provide more detail next time. Jack takes this criticism to mean that he is lazy, and he feels bad.

Everyone "filters" information differently. Many people tend to focus on the areas that they consider to be weaknesses. In the example, Jack thinks he is inadequate, so he looks for things that reinforce this belief. Unfortunately, when Jack's thoughts become negative, he becomes angry. If Jack does not know how to change or control these negative thoughts and unpleasant feelings, he will act them out, often in an aggressive manner.

♦ **Overgeneralization** – This occurs when a person bases his or her conclusion about a situation on only one piece of information or one experience. For example, a boy asks a girl for a Friday night date and she turns him down. From that experience, he concludes that no girl will ever want to go out with him. The boy uses this one incident to conclude that all girls don't like him, and ignores any other evidence to the contrary. Later on, when the boy's mother asks him if he would like to go to a movie on Friday night, he blows up and begins yelling and cursing. The mother has no idea that her son thinks she is teasing him about not having a date.

♦ **Mind-Reading** – In this situation, the youth makes an assumption without having any evidence to support the assumption. An example would be a situation where a teacher asks a child to stay after class for a few minutes. Even though he knows he hasn't done anything wrong, the child immediately thinks, "Man, I'm probably going to get a detention or something." This youth thinks that everyone has the same thoughts and feelings that he has; if he sees the worst in everyone and every situation, he assumes that people feel the same way about him.

♦ **Personalization** – This occurs when a child thinks that everything that happens is related to him or her, and that he or she is responsible for every situation. For example, if a girl's best friend is angry, the girl will assume that she did something to make the friend angry. This child also compares herself with others: "She's prettier than me…,"; I'm not as smart as him…,"; "I'm a better soccer player than her…," and so on. The child sees everything that goes on around her as a measure of her worth. And because she thinks everything is related to her, even the most innocuous event can lead to anger, frustration, disappointment, etc., and an aggressive response. Often, other people don't know how to respond to this aggression because they don't see an incident as being related to the child at all.

♦ **Control Fallacies** – There are two possible ways children can distort their feelings of being in control: They can see themselves as being totally under others' control, or as being totally responsible for everyone around them. The child who feels that everyone else is in control is more likely to be a reactive aggressive child. This child feels that he doesn't have any control over his life, and that he just responds to everyone else's decisions. Because the child feels like everything is being done to him, it is easy for him to be angry with and resentful of those around him. He also feels helpless because he does not think he can influence anything that goes on in his life. This leads to poor decision-making because the child does not think any solution he comes up with is going to matter anyway.

- ◆ **Fallacy of Fairness** – In this situation, children view everything in terms of "fairness," or how much others care for them. A youngster's thinking follows this kind of logic: "If my teacher liked me, she wouldn't give me a 'D'"; "If my parents loved me, they wouldn't make me baby-sit my sister all the time"; "If my girlfriend really cared for me, she'd go out with me Friday, instead of staying home for her sister's birthday." Since no one can live up to this child's expectations, he begins to resent almost everyone with whom he has a relationship. Over time, these feelings of resentment can lead the child to try to punish others or to constantly test a relationship with inappropriate behavior.

- ◆ **Blaming** – When a child distorts her thinking in this way, she blames others for her decisions and responsibilities. An example of this would be a situation where a child "blames" her friend for always wanting to play the same game. The child could insist on playing something different or play with a different friend, but it is easier for her to hold the friend responsible. Another example would be a child who gets upset with his mother for suggesting that he work on his model car. The child does not explain that he is watching an exciting part of a movie; he just assumes she knows this.

- ◆ **Heaven's Reward Fallacy** – Children who view things this way always expect to be "paid back" for something they do. For example, a child helps her mother clean the house and wash the car. Later, when Mom tells the girl that she cannot go to a movie that night because it is not appropriate for a 13-year-old, the child blows up and says, "It's not fair. I did everything you wanted all day. You owe me something." She feels cheated and robbed, and responds by trying to "punish" her mother for "tricking" her.

It is easy to see how children who are experiencing any one of these cognitive distortions (and many aggressive children are prone to several) would begin to see people in a hostile, angry light. These children misread situations, and since other people cannot know their thoughts, no one is able to help the children process information more clearly and accurately.

Often, people whose intentions are neutral or positive are caught off guard by the aggressive child's behavior. They have difficulty "reading" what the child is thinking, which makes the child's behavior seem totally unreasonable and irrational. Because other people are unprepared for the child's aggressive response, they are more likely to respond inappropriately as well.

Helping a Child Change Distorted Thinking

This section will look at several ways caregivers can help children overcome distorted thinking and get better at picking up and accurately translating such cues from others.

- ◆ **Describe the situation or event.** Each time the child engages in aggressive behavior, have him write a description of the event. With younger children, you may want to have them tell you about the event while you write out the simple details. When the child first begins this treatment strategy, it might be helpful to have an adult present while the child is working. Initially, the child may have a difficult time figuring out how the incident relates to others. Most aggressive children develop a view of the world by internally processing events, rather than looking at external factors and considering the views of others. In other words, they think only of themselves and not of others. Talking with the child can help draw out more details, not just a slanted description of what others did to provoke the child.

- **Identify thoughts.** Go over the situation with the child. Help him identify his thoughts, particularly those that occur just before the aggressive behavior. Help the child to recognize distortions that may have occurred. When a distortion is identified, have him write it down, or write it down for him.

- **Change the distortion.** After the child has identified the distortion and written it down, have him rewrite the phrase or sentence without the distortion. Initially, children will need a great deal of guidance to do this. Over time, however, older children should be able to do it by themselves. Once that happens, it's important to reinforce this behavior with positive consequences.

Helping the child to recognize distorted thinking and teaching him to change it can be a big step toward changing his aggressive tendencies. Showing the child how to look at things from another person's perspective by providing "other-centered" rationales, and periodically asking the child how he thinks others feel in a given situation also may prove worthwhile. The idea is to help the child realize that other people have feelings, and that just as the behaviors of others affect him, his behavior affects others.

- **Thought-stopping.** This is a simple process where the child is asked to picture a stop sign inside his head when he has a thought that could lead to aggressive behavior; he then tells himself to "stop" the thought. If you are working with a younger child, explain that he should just picture the stop sign again if the thought returns. With practice, the child eventually will be able to remove himself from the situation or think about other things. Older children can be told to try to replace the negative thought with an alternative positive thought. So if a child is thinking, "Nobody likes me," he should try to think, "Well, some people like me; my friend,

Ron, for instance." The goal is to help the child change the thought before it leads to aggressive behavior.

Earlier, we mentioned that a child's distortions can lead to feelings that may result in aggressive behavior. Often, when we act spontaneously, we are reacting to our emotions. Children are no different. Aggressive children often report feeling anxious, alienated from others, angry, fearful, frustrated, hurt, or inadequate before they display aggressive behavior. Certain situations are more likely to cause these feelings than others. These situations include being teased, getting criticized, receiving consequences, being rejected, being told "No," or having a trust betrayed. These situations are difficult for most of us to deal with, so it is not surprising that a child whose distortions already make him see others as hostile would find them even more challenging.

Using Time-Out

One treatment strategy that works well with young children or kids at lower developmental levels is Time-Out. Time-Out involves having a child sit in one place for a certain amount of time, away from all the enjoyable things in the child's life. Time-Out works with most young kids because they eventually begin to realize that using appropriate behaviors helps them to stay out of Time-Out, allowing them to do things they like to do.

When using this intervention, caregivers should follow these basic guidelines.

- Immediately following a problem behavior, describe the behavior to the child and send (or take) him or her to the Time-Out area. Stay calm and describe the behavior only once. Do not reason, explain, lecture, argue, threaten, raise your voice, or use physical punishment (e.g., spanking). In fact, avoid giving the child a lot of attention at this time.

♦ Choose a convenient place for a Time-Out area. It doesn't have to be the same place each time. A kitchen chair, a couch, a footstool, or a step will work. Make sure the area is safe, well-lit, and away from enjoyable distractions like the TV or radio or toys.

♦ Before you ever begin using Time-Out, explain to the child what it is, which problem behaviors it will be used for, and how long it will last. For example, you could say, "When I ask you to put your toys away and you start crying and throwing your toys, you will have to go sit on a chair in the kitchen for three minutes. I'll start the timer on the stove and when it buzzes you can get up." Then practice having the child go to the chair when you ask.

♦ As a general rule, a child should spend one minute in Time-Out for every year of his or her age. In other words, if a child is five years old, quiet time should last no longer than five minutes. Kids may think it's fun the first time you practice, but it's quite likely they won't enjoy an actual Time-Out situation. Therefore, it's very important to specifically explain the process beforehand and prepare the child for the real thing.

♦ During Time-Out, the child is to sit calmly and quietly in the designated area. If the child complains, makes angry statements, cries, or throws a tantrum, it does not count toward "quiet time." On the other hand, fidgeting and talking in a soft voice can count. Don't start the time until the child is quiet; if you start the time and the child starts to cry or begins a tantrum again, wait until he or she is quiet and start the time over again.

♦ The child must stay seated and quiet during Time-Out. If the child decides not to cooperate and tries to leave, calmly return him or her to the Time-Out area. If this continues (and it often does when you first begin using Time-Out), keep returning the child to the area. If you get tired or other activities take you away from the Time-Out, you can have the child leave the area, but be sure to use a different consequence. The child may lose play time with toys or TV privileges, or friends may have to go home. When the child is calm, practice using Time-Out again so that the child will learn to stay in Time-Out during actual situations.

Early in the process, the child may cry, say nasty things about you, throw objects, or make a mess. Ignore behaviors that are not dangerous to the child, you, or the surroundings. Kids use these negative behaviors to try to get your attention and stop the Time-Out; remember that Time-Out is a time when the child doesn't get any attention.

♦ When the Time-Out is over, ask the child, "Are you ready to get up?" The child must answer in a way that's agreeable to you – a nod or an "Okay" work just fine. Then you can tell the child that time is up and that he or she can leave.

Keep in mind that Time-Out is most effective with younger kids and kids at lower developmental levels. It shouldn't be used with older children or adolescents; for these kids it's usually more effective to deliver a consequence that removes something they like (e.g., loss of phone, TV, or computer privileges, etc.) or adds something they don't like (e.g., extra chore).

Aggression Log

An aggression log is a treatment intervention that can provide youth and caregivers with valuable insight and information about a youth's aggression problem. The log, which is filled out by a youth during a quiet time after an aggressive incident has been resolved, helps track the cause, severity, and frequency of aggressive behaviors. It also is a way for youth to reflect on the thoughts and feelings that go with those behaviors. Over time, youth and caregivers can use the log to identify progress and areas where improvement or more teaching is necessary.

Before caregivers decide to use an aggression log in treatment, they should do a lot of Proactive Teaching with the youth. The youth must understand the purpose of the log, how it is to be completed, and how it fits into the Treatment Plan. Caregivers also must make sure that a youth has the necessary writing skills and the ability to reflect on and analyze his or her behaviors. Youth who are not capable of completing a log might become angry or frustrated by the task, and find the treatment to be more punishing than helpful. Keep in mind that aggression logs work best with older children and adolescents, and are probably not a good intervention for younger children or kids at lower developmental levels.

A youth should enter the information about an aggressive incident in private during a quiet time. Caregivers should allow sufficient time after the incident so that the youth is calm and in control of his or her emotions and behaviors. If a youth is not comfortable with the process the first few times a log is used, a caregiver may have to ask the youth questions and record the youth's answers in the appropriate column.

Figure 1 presents a sample aggression log. The following section will explain the different entries the log contains and how the information can be used to help kids get better.

♦ The areas labeled "Date" and "Time" help monitor when and how often incidents are occurring. This helps the youth and caregivers measure whether a youth is making progress, is staying the same, or is getting worse. It also gives a picture of any patterns of behavior that might be developing. For example, a youth might react with more serious aggressive behavior on days when he has to do a certain chore or has a lot of homework. Identifying these types of patterns enables caregivers to make adjustments in a youth's treatment.

♦ The "Place" and "Who Was Present" entries identify where the aggressive behavior took place and who was around, respectively. For example, most of a youth's aggressive

incidents might occur at school, and be directed at females more often than males. Again, this data can help caregivers detect behavior patterns.

♦ The area labeled "Trigger" is where a youth writes what happened just before he or she responded with aggression. This can provide valuable clues about what antecedents may be contributing to a youth's decision to respond with aggression. For example, one day a youth might write, "Some friends were teasing me about my new haircut" in reference to a fight he had with those friends. The next day, the same youth might have another altercation with a different person, and write "Bobby was rubbing it in that he beat me at basketball." These entries would indicate that the youth is having trouble dealing with teasing, and the caregiver could do more teaching in that area.

♦ The "Thoughts" and "Feelings" entries are where a youth writes down what he or she was thinking just before the aggressive behavior occurred. These responses let caregivers know whether the youth needs help with correctly identifying feelings or changing distorted thinking.

Identifying feelings is an area where many youth will require help. Generally, aggressive kids know three feelings: mad, glad, and sad. Oftentimes, they will mistakenly say they were mad before an aggressive incident when they actually were feeling lonely, frustrated, irritated, or something else. The point here is that in order for kids to learn to appropriately deal with unpleasant feelings, they must be able to correctly recognize and label what they are feeling. This might become a priority in a Treatment Plan.

♦ The "Behaviors" area is where the youth writes down the aggressive behaviors he or she used during the incident. Examples might include, "I yelled and swore"; "I punched Sheila in the back"; or "I threatened to hurt the caregiver." Information in this column helps caregivers gauge the

Figure 1

Sample Aggression Log

Date_____Time_____Place _____

Who Was Present _____

_____

Trigger (What happened before)_____

_____

_____

Thoughts _____

_____

_____

Feelings _____

_____

_____

Behaviors _____

_____

_____

Consequences _____

_____

_____

severity and intensity of a youth's aggressive behavior, and determine whether the child's problems are getting better or worse. For example, if over a five-week period a youth has gone from hitting and kicking during problem situations to yelling and cursing, he or she has made progress. This indicates that the treatment strategies that are in place are working. On the other hand, a deterioration of behavior to more extreme forms of aggression indicates that treatment is falling short and changes are necessary.

♦ The final area is labeled "Consequences." Here, the youth lists the consequences that resulted from his or her aggressive behavior. Caregivers must teach youth that these consequences include not only those that are obvious and personal, like losing privileges or earning an extra work chore, but also those that are more far-reaching, like damaging a relationship, losing a person's trust, or causing physical injury. This enables young people to understand that their aggressive behavior has a destructive and harmful effect on their lives and the lives of others.

Once the youth has completed the entries on the aggression log, the caregiver and youth should discuss the content. The main teaching should focus on how the youth can better deal with similar problems in the future. Afterwards, the youth also should earn a positive consequence; the type and size of the consequence should be based on how thoroughly the youth completed the log and the youth's participation in the discussion. If the youth sees this as a reinforcing event, he or she will be more willing to participate again.

Aggression logs are excellent evaluation tools for measuring the success of or need for change in Treatment Plans. Equally important is their value as self-assessment and self-monitoring tools for the kids who use them. The aggressive youngster can use this activity to reflect on and analyze the many different factors that lead up to and follow an aggressive incident. This is extremely valuable for reactive aggressive kids, who don't usually take the time to stop and think about how their aggression negatively affects them and others.

Individual and Group Therapy

Psychotherapy is a popular type of therapy that is often used as part of a troubled youth's overall Treatment Plan. Psychotherapy is based on "intrapsychic" views of the nature of deviant behavior in youth. Intrapsychic processes are those that are viewed as being responsible for maladjustment in youth. Therapy is primarily directed at helping a youth develop or increase awareness of certain thoughts, feelings, and experiences; the youth then works through these issues with a therapist. Because reactive aggressive youth tend to have problems in these areas, this treatment strategy can be appropriate and effective. As with other treatment strategies, it is necessary for the youth and the therapist to have a strong relationship. Youth who trust their caregivers usually are more open in their expression of important thoughts, feelings, and experiences, which can contribute to efforts to bring about therapeutic change.

Having said that, it is important to point out that psychotherapeutic techniques tend to be relatively nonspecific, making it difficult to judge treatment effects or to replicate psychotherapeutic procedures. Consequently, the outcome evidence regarding psychotherapy is not strong enough to determine the effectiveness of psychotherapeutic treatment modalities. Although individual psychotherapists may experience clinical success in treatment, there is little evidence that individual or group psychotherapy alone impacts aggressive behavior (Kazdin, 1985). Kazdin's review of the psychotherapeutic literature indicated that relatively few studies focused specifically on the treatment of aggressive youth and adolescents. In general, intrapsychic approaches are laden with untested theory, both in the development of aggression and the key variables necessary to treat it. However, the value of psychotherapy as part of an overall Treatment Plan for reactive aggressive youth should not be underestimated nor discounted.

Pharmacotherapy

Pharmacotherapy involves the use of various drugs (e.g., stimulants, antidepressants, antimanics, etc.) to control aggression in children and adolescents. This therapy is based on evidence that suggests that for some youth, there may be a biological basis to their aggressive behavior. Our experience at Boys Town has been that reactive aggressive kids are more likely to have medication as part of their overall Treatment Plan than proactive aggressive kids.

To date, there is no established drug treatment that can be broadly applied to treating aggressive behavior in youth. This is due, in part, to the fact that aggression is correlated with a wide variety of other nonbiological attributes (e.g., family history, sex, age, etc.). However, certain classes of drugs such as stimulants and antidepressants have been effective with some aggressive youth.

The use of pharmacotherapy as a treatment strategy for aggression is worth exploring for some specific types of aggressive youth, including those who tend to use reactive aggression. However, pharmacotherapy should be used with other nondrug therapies. In addition, due to the short- and long-term side effects of certain drugs, pharmacotherapy as a treatment for youth should be carried out only under the direct supervision of a professional who has been clinically trained to evaluate, diagnose, prescribe, and monitor psychotropic medications for children and adolescents.

Sample Treatment Plans

Now, let's put all this together. This section contains sample Treatment Plans for two reac-

tive aggressive kids who are being treated in different settings. The first example takes place in a Treatment Foster Care setting, while the second occurs in a psychiatric environment. Each example includes a short summary of the youngster's behavioral history and a completed Treatment Plan.

The information in each summary is the result of a thorough and careful evaluation. The treatment strategies appear in bold face type and targeted skills appear in bold italic type so that you can see how these skills and strategies can be incorporated into a Treatment Plan.

Example 1

Susie is a 10-year-old girl who has been placed in a treatment foster home. The Treatment Parents have a 15-year-old son at home. Susie has been in and out of various placements since she was 3; this is her fifth out-of-home placement. Her history includes placement in two different psychiatric hospitals for a total of four months, placement in a regular foster home for two years, and a three-month stay at an emergency shelter. Susie has lived at home in between these placements. Susie's primary referral problem is aggression toward others; she also has been sexually abused by her mother's boyfriend and has experienced academic difficulties and depression. The Treatment Parents have observed that Susie has great difficulty controlling her aggression. They report that Susie "loses it" without warning when she doesn't like what someone tells her or when she can't have something she wants. When Susie loses self-control, she slams doors, yells and curses, and occasionally hits others. Susie also frequently forgets to close the door when she is in the bathroom. Furthermore, she makes sexual jokes, talks about sexually explicit movies her mother has allowed her to see, and stands too close to people when they are talking. Susie's Treatment Plan follows.

Treatment Plan

Date _____
(first Treatment Plan)

Youth: Susie   **System:** Modified Motivation/Sticker Chart

Problem at Admission: Aggressive Behavior

Target Behavior: (1) Controlling Emotions: *Staying Calm*

Baseline: Frequency of Problem Behavior: 5 per day (average)

Problem Definition

When Susie is angry, frustrated, or upset, she tends to suddenly lose self-control. Generally, this happens when she is told something she doesn't want to hear or when she can't have or do something she wants. During this time, she slams doors, throws things, and sometimes hits others. She also swears, refuses to listen to adults, tells them to "shut up," and refuses to follow instructions.

Goal: Frequency of Problem Behavior: 2 per day (0 per day for physical aggression)

Goal: % of Teaching to Alternative Behaviors: 50% per week

Treatment Strategies

Proactive Teaching

Susie will practice and review the steps of two **self-control strategies** that have been developed for her every day before and after school, and every morning and afternoon on weekends. The strategies are:

1. **Deep-breathing** (take a deep breath in through the nose and hold it for about two seconds, let the breath out slowly through the mouth, repeat this process two or three times until calmed down, when calm tell an adult).

2. **Muscle relaxation** (clench fists and relax them, shake arms for 10 seconds, roll head from side to side).

When Susie has mastered these two strategies, she will begin working on others, including:

1. **Self-talk.**

2. **Telling someone she trusts what is bothering her** (using the skill of *Expressing Feelings Appropriately*).

3. **Problem-solving.**

Susie will be given an opportunity to review or practice the steps to her **self-control strategies** prior to situations where she frequently loses control. Susie will earn one sticker a day for role-playing her **self-control strategies** twice. She also will earn a sticker each day she doesn't lose self-control. At the end of each week, Susie can exchange these stickers for:

♦ a candy bar (seven stickers).

♦ staying up an extra 30 minutes on a nonschool night (10 stickers).

♦ 30 minutes of playing with the Game Boy® (12 stickers).

♦ a video rental and eating popcorn during the movie (14 stickers).

Social Skill Instruction

Susie will earn stickers for using her **self-control strategies** at home and at school. Susie will earn a **Time-Out** and/or lose privileges for not using the skill of *Expressing Feelings Appropriately*. When this happens, Susie can earn back some of her privileges by role-playing the skill of *Expressing Feelings Appropriately*. Susie will lose from one to five stickers when she loses self-control. **Effective Praise, Corrective Teaching,** and **Crisis Teaching** will be used.

Family Meeting

There will be a Family Meeting at least twice during the first week Susie is in the home, and as often as needed each week after that. During these meetings, any problems that any of the children in the home are having with physical aggression will be discussed. (It is important not to "single out" Susie during these meetings, and not to discuss her private treatment issues in public.)

Relationship Development

The Treatment Parents will use **Effective Praise** to help Susie recognize when she is using the steps of her **self-control strategies.** The Treatment Parents will look for opportunities to praise Susie for using the steps of her **self-control strategies.** Susie will be given rationales for how these strategies will benefit her at home, at school, and during visits with her family.

Medication and Individual Therapy

Susie will continue to see Dr. Smith twice a month for **individual therapy** and to monitor her **medication.**

Example 2

Tom is a 13-year-old boy who has a learning disability. He has recently been placed in a residential treatment facility, his sixth different placement since he was 8. Tom displays little impulse control and tends to be overly active and "scattered" in situations that involve groups (e.g., classrooms, group therapy sessions, unit outings, etc.). Tom is easily distracted and overstimulated, and frequently loses his orientation and focus on tasks. The other kids on the unit dislike Tom, and he has great difficulty in his relationships with adults. For example, Tom is likely to argue when someone corrects his behavior, has a hard time completing tasks, and often engages in activities without asking permission. Tom frequently loses self-control and claims that he is "picked on" and treated unfairly by other kids and caregivers on the unit. When he loses self-control, Tom becomes physically aggressive, damages property, and eventually becomes self-injurious. On two occasions during his last three-month placement in a group home setting, Tom lost self-control and cut his arms and hands with glass from windows he broke. Both situations involved an argument with another youth in which a caregiver initially intervened and gave Tom a consequence for his part in the fight. During these two occasions, Tom alternated between threatening to kill himself and the caregiver. The self-inflicted cuts to his arms were serious enough to require stitches and could have been fatal had there not been immediate intervention. Tom has not destroyed property or hurt himself at school; however, one reason for his placement in a more-restrictive psychiatric setting was because he hit a teacher.

Comprehensive Treatment Plan
Residential Treatment Center

Date of Admission: January 1

Name: Tom   Date of Initial Treatment Plan: January 10

Medical Record Number: 00-00-00

Priority Treatment List

Priority Yes	No	Problem List
X		History of self-harm statements and attempts.
X		Acts out aggressively (including assault).
X		Difficulty expressing feelings appropriately.
X		Symptoms of depression (e.g., withdrawn, tearful, easily distracted, low self-esteem).
X		Poor coping skills.
X		Family relationship issues.
X		Poor anger/impulse control.
X		Difficulty accepting decisions of authority.
X		Behind on school credits.
	X	History of drug and alcohol use – The other placements report that, to the best of their knowledge, Tom has not used drugs or alcohol in the last year.

Each "No" response requires a rationalization to be listed following the problem.

Comprehensive Treatment Plan

Date of Admission: January 1

Medication: Zoloft (50 mg.) in the morning.

Goal : Tom will decrease self-harm statements and self-injurious behaviors while increasing his ability to *express feelings appropriately.**

Objective #1: Tom will increase his ability to *express his feelings appropriately* to a rate of 90% as measured across all areas by February 15.

_____ **Date Achieved**

Objective #2: Tom will increase his ability to *express feelings appropriately* regarding family issues in **individual, family, and group therapy** to a rate of 90% as measured across all areas by February 15.

_____ **Date Achieved**

Objective #3: Tom will increase his ability to use *positive self-statements* to a rate of 90% as measured across all areas by February 15.

_____ **Date Achieved**

Objective #4: Tom will increase his ability to *participate in activities* to a rate of 90% as measured across all areas by February 15.

_____ **Date Achieved**

Persons Responsible: Doug Smith, MD; Dawn Johnson, MSW; Rick Doe, Unit Coordinator

*See the Boys Town manual, ***Teaching Social Skills to Youth,*** for the steps of the skills listed in the Comprehensive Treatment Plan.

Tom
DOB 6/17/xx
M.R. # 00-00-00

Goal: Tom will decrease his aggression while increasing his ability to *accept decisions of authority.*

Objective #1: Tom will increase his ability to *accept decisions of authority* to the rate of 90% as measured across all areas by February 15.

_____ **Date Achieved**

Objective #2: Tom will reduce the number of aggressive incidents (i.e., assaults) to zero for 30 days by February 15.

_____ **Date Achieved**

Objective #3: Tom will increase his ability to *control emotions* and deal with frustration and anger to a rate of 90% by using his *self-control strategies* of **deep-breathing** and **visual imagery** and an **aggression log** by February 15.

_____ **Date Achieved**

Persons Responsible: Doug Smith, MD; Dawn Johnson, MSW; Rick Doe, Unit Coordinator

Goal: Tom will improve confidence and competence in his academic abilities and study skills.

Objective #1: Tom will remain on task when directed and demonstrate this by *accepting help or assistance, asking for help,* and *participating in activities* in the classroom in four out of seven class periods by February 15.

_____ **Date Achieved**

Objective #2: Tom will *complete tasks* (i.e., school assignments) at 80% accuracy in five out of seven class periods by February 15.

_____ **Date Achieved**

Objective #3: Tom will *spontaneously problem-solve* with peers and staff when conflicts arise in the classroom in four out of seven class periods by February 19.

_____ **Date Achieved**

Objective #4: Tom will attempt to be more *assertive* and *resist peer pressure* in four out of seven class periods by February 19.

_____ **Date Achieved**

Person Responsible: Cathy Wilson, MA

Comprehensive Treatment Plan Review

Treatment Strategies: **Individual, group**, and **family therapy** using cognitive-behavioral strategies, family system strategies, level system, therapeutic milieu, and medications.

Data Collection: Weekly medical chart probes, professional observation, and motivation system card data.

Treatment Team Reviews

Review 1: Date: February 17

During this review period, Tom has made minimal progress on all objectives. He has engaged in nine incidents of physical aggression and has been physically assaultive toward peers and staff on four occasions. Tom also has made five self-harm statements and engaged in two incidents of self-destructive behavior. Due to these statements and behaviors, Dr. Smith placed Tom on suicide evaluation on three separate occasions. A new objective will be designed so that the occurrences of these statements and behaviors can continue to be monitored and measured. The treatment team will meet within 24 hours to discuss and disseminate the new objective.

Review 2: Date: _____

Review 3: Date: _____

Review 4: Date: _____

Discharge Plan

Estimated length of stay: Three to four months.

Criteria For Discharge: No incidents of aggression for 30 days.

Projected Placement: Group living environment.

Transition: 15-30 days.

Psychiatric Consultation: Ongoing for monitoring **medications** and mental health needs.

Therapy: **Individual** and **group sessions** with unit therapist.

Medical: None.

Other: Parents will attend and complete a Boys Town Common Sense Parenting® course.

Treatment Team Reviews

Review 1: Date: February 17

Review of Discharge Plan and Reason for Continued Care:

During this review period, Tom has had several behavioral difficulties within the classroom setting; this environment seems to be a great source of frustration. Tom also has had difficulty *controlling his anger* impulses and has made several self-harm statements instead of *expressing his feelings appropriately*. Continued practice, effort, and improvement is needed before Tom will be able to move to a less-restrictive level of care.

Tom's parents are enrolled in and will attend a Boys Town Common Sense Parenting course next month.

Review 2: Date: _____

Review of Discharge Plan and Reason for Continued Care:

Review 3: Date: _____

Review of Discharge Plan and Reason for Continued Care:

Summary

Every youth who receives treatment deserves and requires individualized treatment. This can be accomplished through the use of a comprehensive evaluation of a youngster's problem. From that evaluation, a Treatment Plan can be developed that includes interventions designed specifically to treat the youth's aggression problem. Children and adolescents who use reactive aggression have a unique set of issues and problems that require special attention and treatment. Some strategies that have proven effective for these kids include social skill instruction, changing cognitive distortions, aggression logs, individual and group therapy, medications, and others. Remember, however, that the therapeutic power of a Treatment Plan lies not in each strategy alone, but in the sum of the values of all interventions.

CHAPTER 10
Treatment Strategies for Proactive Aggression

The major payoff for proactive aggressive kids is acquiring things. They bully, control, or dominate to get what they want, regardless of whether others are hurt in the process. The proactive aggressive child uses aggression like a tool; he or she has learned to manipulate others by using verbal or physical attacks. This type of aggression is more thought out and calculating, and less emotional, so the youth may or may not be angry, upset, or experiencing any unpleasant feelings. Thus, one of the major goals during the treatment planning process should be to target skills that teach these kids sensitivity toward others and how to build healthy, lasting relationships.

This chapter will focus on some of the treatment interventions that Boys Town has found effective in helping caregivers achieve treatment goals for proactive aggressive children and adolescents. Also included are sample Treatment Plans for two proactive aggressive youth in two different settings.

Keep in mind that the following strategies in and of themselves are not meant to be "cure-alls" for proactive aggression. When putting together an effective and therapeutic Treatment Plan, caregivers should carefully evaluate and choose a variety of these interventions.

Social Skill Instruction

Social skill instruction is a powerful and effective intervention for treating proactive aggression. But several key issues should be incorporated into your teaching to help enhance its effectiveness and therapeutic value. These issues are discussed here.

Focus on the Positive

When working with proactive aggressive youth, it is important to change certain patterns that have developed and contributed to the continuation of negative behavior. One such pattern involves situations where children have received no praise or attention for positive behaviors, and are noticed (and punished) only when they use aggression. After a while, these kids turn exclusively to aggressive behaviors to get attention and other things they want.

Focusing on catching these kids being good, praising, and reinforcing positive behavior through lots of Effective Praise is one important way to break this pattern. Believe it or not, these kids will engage in prosocial skills while in your care. In the beginning, it generally will be something very small and inconspicuous, such as not making a negative comment to or teasing another youth, or picking up another child's fork from the floor during dinner.

Caregivers may have to look long and hard for these kinds of opportunities to praise kids. But it's a place to start! Remember, the goal is to teach these kids skills that will help them become sensitive to others and interact with adults and kids in appropriate, friendly ways. Including a lot of Effective Praise in a Treatment Plan helps proactive aggressive kids see the rewards and benefits that come from using positive behaviors. Over time, with plenty of determination and patience from caregivers, these kids will begin to realize that they can get their needs met in positive ways, and will become less and less dependent on their old aggressive behaviors.

Effective Praise also allows a caregiver to show an aggressive child how to respond to others in a positive fashion. Caregivers model the qualities and skills needed to teach these kids sensitivity toward others and how to build and maintain a positive relationship. For many kids, the real-life demonstration you provide as part of Effective Praise may be the catalyst they need to begin making the necessary changes in their lives.

A final benefit of frequently using Effective Praise (along with other relationship development strategies) in a Treatment Plan is that it strengthens your relationship with the child. Over time, the child begins to like the positive attention, and seeks to please you instead of disappoint you. As kids begin to see that you are truly concerned about them, they start to use more of the positive, prosocial behaviors that you have taught them.

Use All the Teaching Interactions

Proactive aggressive youngsters respond very well to the contingencies and consequences that are built into Corrective Teaching and Crisis Teaching. Kids who are calculating in their use of aggression are better able to understand that there are negative consequences attached to their aggressive actions. Unfortunately, if you let an aggressive act pass by without responding with Corrective Teaching or Crisis Teaching, you are likely to see that same aggressive behavior again. Therefore, caregivers need to address and teach to every incident of aggressive behavior when it occurs.

Proactive Teaching also can contribute to the effectiveness of a Treatment Plan. This type of teaching can be extremely effective with proactive aggressive kids and should be used frequently, especially when a child is new to a program. During these teaching sessions, focus on making your expectations clear, and consistently give consequences (both positive and negative) when a child meets or fails to meet those expectations. This not only sets the child up for success, but also shows him or her that you are fair, and strengthens the relationship.

Stay the Course

"I'm gonna kick your a-- if you don't let me have that!"

"Why are you always so unfair to me? I want to call my mom!"

"You son of a b----! I hate your guts!"

"You don't like me! You're just like all the others who treat me like s---!"

— ◆ —

Proactive aggressive kids are masters at using verbal statements like these. The intent here usually is to bait a caregiver into a frivolous argument or a fruitless discussion that will sidetrack the caregiver's teaching and draw attention away from the youth's aggressive behavior. When kids attempt to do this, caregivers must not get "sucked in." Remember, this is only a ploy kids use to avoid or escape negative consequences they've earned for inappropriate behavior.

It is tempting to want to respond to "baiting" statements when they happen. But a good rule of thumb is to ignore them or simply acknowledge the child's concerns by saying you would be happy to talk about them later. Above all, stay focused on your teaching. Once a youngster has calmed down, you can follow up on any concerns or problems he or she brings up. During Corrective Teaching and Crisis Teaching it is important to keep the focus on the child's aggressive behavior.

Many caregivers make the mistake of taking these statements personally. This causes them to react in an emotional manner and suddenly, caregivers find themselves defending or explaining what they said instead of finishing their teaching. To avoid this situation during Corrective Teaching or Crisis Teaching, stay calm and keep the responsibility squarely on the child's behavior, not yours. When you follow up with the child later, you usually will find that the youngster either forgot about what he or she said or no longer believes it is important.

Do More than Choose the Right Skills

When choosing social skills for Treatment Plans for proactive aggressive children and adolescents, it is important to always keep the primary treatment goals in mind. These kids need to learn the skills that relate to the concepts of getting along with others and building healthy relationships. This might include teaching skills like *Volunteering, Making an Apology, Compromising with Others, Showing Sensitivity to Others,* and so on. (See Appendix A, "Social Skills for Aggressive Youth," for more examples of social skills for proactive aggressive kids.)

In addition to assigning appropriate skills as part of a child's overall Treatment Plan,

there are many other creative ways to go about teaching these concepts. For example, you can take youth to homeless shelters to help serve meals, to homes for senior citizens or veterans to spend time with residents, or to a women's shelter to read stories to the young children. Kids also can volunteer for community projects like neighborhood clean-ups, painting houses or cleaning yards for the elderly or economically disadvantaged, food drives, and many others.

The point here is that proactive aggressive kids must learn to stop focusing on themselves and turn their attention to others. Choosing and using the right social skills is one way to accomplish this. But if you take it one step further by incorporating many types of real-life activities into a child's Treatment Plan, kids can learn very powerful and influential lessons about what it really means to put others ahead of themselves.

Work Chores

Because many proactive aggressive youth understand that there are negative ramifications to their aggression, work chores are effective consequences to incorporate into a Treatment Plan. Work chores require a child to sacrifice time and effort that could be spent playing or doing something enjoyable. And the process of adding work chores is simple. Take, for example, a situation where an older boy has verbally threatened a younger boy in order to get his candy. As you begin to use Corrective Teaching, the older boy begins arguing and making excuses. Once he calms down, you finish the Corrective Teaching Interaction and deliver a consequence (e.g., loss of privilege related to the behavior) for making threats. Then you can add the work chore of helping to clean the bathroom for arguing with you. Both consequences should be effective at reducing those behavior problems in the future.

In some instances, a chore can relate directly to the problem behavior. For example, if a youngster knocks over a couple of kitchen chairs during a tantrum, a good work chore might be having the youth straighten up the rest of the kitchen after he picks up the chairs.

Here are some examples of how work chores can be used as consequences for aggressive kids.

♦ A girl breaks another youngster's radio. To make restitution, she must do chores to earn money to buy the other child a new radio.

♦ A boy steals another child's video game. Later, the boy wants to call his best friend. As a consequence for stealing, you decide that the youth has to do the other child's daily chore as well as his own daily chore before he can make the call.

♦ A girl is yelling at another youth to get off the phone so she can make a call. Her consequence is folding a load of laundry that the other child was supposed to fold as a regular chore.

♦ A boy pushes another child to the floor during an argument over whose turn it is to put away the clean dishes. As a consequence for his aggressive behavior, the boy has to put away the dishes for the next three days.

Here is a list of work chores that can be added as consequences, where possible. Add chores in areas that are different from the chores kids do as part of their daily routine.

Folding laundry

Putting laundry away

Making another child's bed

Vacuuming

Raking all or part of the yard

Mowing the grass

Taking out the trash

Collecting the trash from throughout the house

Helping another youth with his or her chores

Dusting furniture

Sweeping the porch

Washing some or all of the windows

Washing the car

Vacuuming the carpet in the car

Washing the car windows

Cleaning the garage

Helping a youth put toys away

Washing, drying, or putting away the dishes

Sweeping the kitchen (dining room) floor

Cleaning the bathroom

Cleaning the kitchen sink

Cleaning the bedroom

Shaking the rugs

It's up to caregivers to decide how often a chore should be done, and to define exactly what the child should do. Take into account the age and ability of the child. Also, adjust the consequences to fit the severity of the problem behavior. Remember to use the smallest consequence necessary to change the behavior.

One variation in this area is the chore jar. Here, caregivers write different chores on small pieces of paper and put them in the jar. When a child engages in an aggressive act, the child must select a chore from the jar. This is easier for caregivers because the consequences are made up ahead of time and are readily available. It's important that caregivers tell kids ahead of time about the chore jar and how it will work. Caregivers can use a chore jar for less severe aggressive behaviors like noncompliance, arguing, sarcasm, and so on.

Problem-Solving

The aggressive youth has learned a pattern of behavior that is self-destructive and self-defeating with respect to successful community living. This pattern of behavior is played out daily in every facet of the youth's life (e.g., home, school, and work) and results in numerous interpersonal confrontations. Research has shown that aggressive youth usually interpret interpersonal encounters as hostile and are less sensitive to interpersonal conflict (Kazdin, 1985). Additionally, they generate fewer alternative solutions to interpersonal encounters than other youth and their solutions are almost always aggressive in nature. While caregivers should actively intervene when confrontations occur and teach the youth alternative behavior patterns, the ultimate goal is to help youth develop effective skills that they can use on their own to avoid confrontations.

Problem-solving is one of those skills. This step-by-step process enables youth to accurately identify a problem, come up with options, review the pros and cons of each option, and finally reach a solution.

The next sections will discuss various aspects and benefits of problem solving and a problem-solving method known as **SODAS**.

Problem-Solving Counseling

Problem-solving counseling involves actively teaching an aggressive youth how to explore his or her feelings and develop more appropriate responses to these feelings. Such counseling can help youth learn to think through an issue before making a decision and can provide caregivers with the opportunity to guide the decision-making process.

Caregivers should not appear shocked by anything an aggressive youth might say. It is very important for you to accept a youth's feelings and let him or her know that it's okay to express these feelings to you. This helps the youth feel comfortable about expressing emo-

tions, fears, and concerns about intimate or embarrassing events. This also helps caregivers to better understand the youth and to assess his or her current behavior in the context of those feelings.

In the Boys Town Teaching Model, problem-solving counseling goes beyond the traditional exploration of feelings and seeks to help youth work out new, more appropriate ways to express them. The message here for youth is that it's okay to feel a certain way, but it's not okay to behave any way you want. Society holds us accountable for what we do.

Goals of Problem-Solving

A caregiver's goals during problem-solving counseling sessions are to help the aggressive youth arrive at a viable solution to his or her problem and to teach the youth problem-solving skills. Because such counseling sessions also promote and establish trust between the caregiver and the youth, another benefit is the opportunity to build relationships during such sessions through expressions of concern, affection, respect, and interest in the youth's problems. As an aggressive youth confides in you and sees that you respond with respect, concern, and helpfulness, he or she will feel more and more comfortable problem solving with you in the future.

When to Use Problem-Solving

Problem-solving counseling is most appropriate when an aggressive youth needs to develop a plan to deal with a problem. The problem may be one that he or she is currently experiencing or one that is anticipated, and might involve the youth's parents, siblings, teachers, friends, employer, girlfriend, or boyfriend. Such problems can range from how to talk with an employer whom the youth feels is unfair, to how to resist peer pressure, to deciding whether to participate in an activity. Problem solving also can be used retrospectively to help a youth make a better decision in the future. For example, a caregiver may help an aggressive youth review a problem that resulted in a fight at school and arrive at a more acceptable solution to a similar future situation.

There are some situations when problem-solving counseling is not appropriate. These can include times when a caregiver is attempting to teach an aggressive youth a new skill, or is dealing with inappropriate behaviors such as skill deficiencies, rule violations, or inattentive ongoing negative behavior. Such youth behaviors should be consistently addressed with Proactive Teaching and Corrective Teaching. At times, caregivers may be tempted to counsel when a youth is passive and withdrawn or when the child complains about unfairness. In such cases, it is important to stay on task, regain the youth's attention and cooperation, and complete the necessary teaching. Later, when the youth is calm and his or her behavior is appropriate, the caregiver may choose to initiate a problem-solving counseling session.

When serious issues arise, caregivers should seek professional guidance from a therapist. For example, you can help a youth through a divorce or a death in his or her family. But you must recognize that these events can be so traumatic that the youth might need counseling from a therapist who specializes in this area. Another example of a time when professional help is needed is when a youth threatens to commit suicide. Suicide threats should always be taken seriously and a supervisor or therapist should be consulted immediately.

Caregivers also should not attempt counseling when a youth is under the influence of drugs or alcohol. If a youth is intoxicated, he or she will be incapable of good decision-making. Counseling may even provoke violent behavior from an aggressive youth. Therefore, there should be no counseling or consequences until the youth is sober.

Caregiver Counseling Behaviors

The following qualities are critical for effective and successful problem-solving counseling with aggressive youth. Mastering these qualities requires practice and reflection, and will enhance your effectiveness in working with aggressive youth.

♦ **Listening skills** – Caregivers who have good listening skills are better able to encourage the youth to discuss issues and express feelings and thoughts. A caregiver can indicate that he or she cares about and respects what the youth is saying by looking at him or her, not interrupting, frequently nodding, and generally being attentive.

♦ **Verbal behavior** – Caregivers can keep an aggressive youth focused on the subject and involved by offering verbal encouragement and praise (e.g., "It's really good that you're thinking this through."). Asking clarifying questions and requesting more information will encourage the youth to participate even more (e.g., "Tell me a little more about what happened after that.").

♦ **Empathy** – Providing empathy during the discussion lets the youth know that you are trying to understand the youth's feelings and point of view (e.g., "That must be very upsetting to you" or "It looks like you're really angry about that."). Empathy is very important in establishing rapport with an aggressive youth and encouraging him or her to discuss issues.

♦ **Physical proximity** – Caregivers should avoid sitting behind a desk or table, or having other physical barriers between them and the youth. This can make caregivers appear to be less open and accessible to the youth. Sitting on a couch with a youth or sitting in a chair directly across from him or her establishes a relaxed and comfortable setting for the youth.

While all these qualities are important to facilitate problem-solving, they also should be used in your day-to-day interactions with each youth. Caregivers need to express care and concern, listen, offer empathy, and be open any time they are working with or talking to a youth. Nurturing and caring occurs daily. When caregivers consistently express their concern and act in ways that demonstrate their commitment, aggressive youth are more likely to come to them with problems.

Problem-Solving Procedures

Caregivers guide the counseling and rational problem-solving process by using the **SODAS** method, a revision of a counseling process developed by Jan Roosa (1973). SODAS is an acronym that stands for the following steps:

S Define the problem **situation**.

O Examine **options** available to deal with the problem.

D Determine the **disadvantages** of each option.

A Determine the **advantages** of each option.

S Decide on the **solution/simulation**.

While using the SODAS method, caregivers should use all the supportive nonverbal and verbal behaviors previously discussed. Each of the SODAS components is explained in more detail on the following pages.

Situation

The problem-solving process begins with the caregiver helping the aggressive youth clearly define the situation or problem. In some cases the youth initially will present vague and emotional descriptions (e.g., "I'm sick of school" or "My folks don't care what happens to me."). Caregivers can use general

clarifying questions or statements to help the youth more fully describe the issues (e.g., "Why don't you explain that some more."). However, it may be necessary to ask direct, specific questions (e.g., "Why are you sick of school?" or "Did something happen during your home visit?"). By calmly and skillfully asking these questions, caregivers can keep the youth involved and help the youth articulate a realistic description of the situation.

As questions are asked and the youth responds, the caregiver should provide empathy, concern, and encouragement. Without empathy, concern, and encouragement statements, the questions can become more of an interrogation that could cause the youth to withdraw.

As the youth more clearly defines the situation, the caregiver should summarize what the youth is saying. This summarization is particularly important before any options are discussed. The summarization helps assure that all relevant information has been reviewed and that the caregiver has an accurate picture of the youth's situation. If the summarization is inaccurate or incomplete, the youth has the opportunity to correct any misperceptions. This is especially important at this point since the remainder of the process is built around the defined situation. Without an accurate or clearly defined situation, it will be difficult to generate useful options and a viable solution.

Options

After the situation is clearly defined, the caregiver helps the youth generate options for solving the problem. It is important to have the aggressive youth generate these possible solutions since the goal is to have the youth develop the ability to solve problems on his or her own.

To help the youth generate options, the caregiver should specifically ask the youth how he or she might solve the problem or deal with the situation (e.g., "Can you think of a way to handle that?" or "What do you think you can do about this?"). After the youth suggests an option, the caregiver should continue to solicit additional options (e.g., "Can you think of any other ideas?").

Initially, a youth may have difficulty generating options. The suggestions he or she offers may not be very helpful or realistic. Whenever a youth does come up with an option, the caregiver should remain nonjudgmental and make a positive comment about the youth's participation in the process (e.g., "Well good, you've come up with a second option. You're really trying to think this through."). The caregiver also can offer a neutral comment and a prompt for more options (e.g., "Okay, that's one option. Can you think of another one?").

Remaining nonjudgmental can be difficult for caregivers, especially when the aggressive youth suggests an option that would only result in greater difficulties (e.g., "I'll just have to punch him out."). The caregiver should remember that his or her role at this point is just to get the youth to generate options. In that sense, this phase of the process is a "brainstorming" session. If a caregiver discounts or denies the youth an opportunity to come up with options, it may harm the relationship with the youth and may diminish the likelihood that the youth will come to the caregiver with problems. (During the next phase of examining the advantages and disadvantages, the caregiver can help the youth judge the "wisdom" of the suggested options.)

After the youngster has given all of his or her ideas, a caregiver may give his or her suggestions as well. Options should be phrased as questions (e.g., "How about talking to the teacher after class?") so that the youth still feels involved in the process. Over time, aggressive youth will be better able to generate options and will be more comfortable doing so.

Disadvantages and Advantages

After a number of options have been generated, the caregiver helps the youth think through and discuss the disadvantages and advantages of each one. In a sense, the caregiver is trying to teach the aggressive youth that there is a cause-and-effect relationship between making decisions and what happens to him or her.

As in generating options, it is important that the youth come up with some advantages and disadvantages. Again, the caregiver's role is to skillfully guide the youth by asking general questions (e.g., "Can you think of any problems if you do that?" or "Are there any benefits for doing that?"). If the youth has difficulty thinking of the disadvantages and advantages, the caregiver can help by asking more specific questions (e.g., "Well, what do you think your teacher will do if you start a fight in his class?" or "Do you think she might be more willing to listen to you if you did that?").

There may be a number of disadvantages and advantages for any given option. Since a goal is to help the youth learn to think, it is important to solicit as many disadvantages and advantages as possible (e.g., "Can you think of any other advantages? Any other problems?"). Caregivers should remain nonjudgmental and not argue with the youth about his or her perceptions of the disadvantages and advantages. This can be difficult when the youth is enthusiastic about the advantages of an option that may be unrealistic or problematic (e.g., "Yeah, it'd be great to fight it out because then he'd leave me alone and everybody would think I was bad."). Rather than argue about an advantage, the caregiver can simply acknowledge the youth's view (e.g., "Okay, so you think that an advantage would be....") and guide the youth's judgment during the discussion of the disadvantages (e.g., "What happens if you don't win?"; "Could you get hurt?"; or "What will your boss do if he hears you've fought with another employee?").

If the youth clearly does not see or cannot be directed to verbalize an important advantage or disadvantage, caregivers should offer their viewpoint and allow the youth to react.

The caregiver can finish this step by summarizing each option and its advantages and disadvantages. This summary further helps the youth see the cause-and-effect relationships.

Solution/Simulation

In this step, the youth selects a solution and prepares to successfully implement it by practicing. Typically, as a result of examining disadvantages and advantages, the youth selects a workable option. It may not always be the best option in the caregiver's opinion, but it must belong to the youth. If the youth feels some ownership of the choice, he or she is more likely to be committed to making the option work.

After the youth has selected an option, the caregiver should provide encouragement and reassurance that the youth can successfully implement the solution. Caregivers also can help make the youth comfortable with the solution by answering any questions the youth may have about how to use it.

Another important aspect of improving the youth's chance for success is setting up a role-play or practice session. These role-play sessions should be as realistic as possible. Often, caregivers will know the people the youth will interact with as he or she implements the solutions (e.g., parents, friends, employers, teacher). Because they know the individual(s), they can behave like those people. For example, if an employer is fairly abrupt and somewhat stern, a caregiver can best help the youth by portraying the employer in that manner. The caregiver can make the role-play more realistic by giving the youth several different responses; this can help prepare the youth for the unexpected.

Caregivers should express confidence in the aggressive youth's ability to implement the solution. However, they should not promise the youngster that the solution will work. As the practice session ends, caregivers should prompt the youth to check back after he or she has tried to implement the solution. If the youth succeeds, caregivers should praise the child for doing so and for going through the problem-solving session. If the solution does not work, caregivers should be supportive and empathetic. Caregivers and aggressive youth can then return to the SODAS format to find another solution.

SODAS is an appropriate and effective intervention for both proactive and reactive aggression. With proactive aggressive kids, this problem-solving approach will most likely be a primary intervention; that is why it is included and discussed in this chapter. The SODAS process teaches proactive aggressive kids to become more empathetic and to begin thinking about how their aggression negatively affects others. In addition, these kids learn how to generate options that are nonaggressive, and how to improve rather than damage relationships. These, if you recall, are the main treatment goals for proactive aggression.

The principal treatment goal for reactive aggressive kids is to learn to stop their explosive reactions before they happen and to control their behaviors by using calming techniques (i.e., self-control strategies). This will take a lot of time and effort, but once reactive aggressive kids have demonstrated they can do this, caregivers can add the SODAS problem-solving process to their Treatment Plans. Simply put, this problem-solving method is a higher level skill for reactive aggressive kids that can and should be taught once the fundamental treatment goals are reached.

Learning to problem-solve is a complex task, but it is critical to an aggressive youth's eventual success. It is so important that a youth can earn some type of reward to reinforce his or her cooperation and participation. Further, because aggressive youth have "solved" their problems in inappropriate ways in the past (e.g., running away, becoming angry), it is important to praise a youth when he or she indicates a desire to talk about a problem (e.g., "I have a problem at work. Can you talk with me about it?").

Using the entire SODAS process during a private counseling session is important in teaching rational problem-solving skills to aggressive youth. However, there are many other types of informal and formal ways to model and directly teach this problem-solving approach. For example, a caregiver and youth may be riding in a van together and observe a young person speed through an intersection, run a red light, and squeal his car's tires. At that point, the aggressive youth may say that she can hardly wait until she can have a car and be "bad." The caregiver could use this opportunity to ask the youth if she sees any problems (disadvantages) with running red lights or speeding. The caregiver also could ask the youth for ideas (options) about how to impress people with a car without engaging in unsafe or illegal activities. Such informal discussions can help aggressive youth learn to think ahead, get their needs met in appropriate ways, and connect their actions with future possible consequences. All these behaviors are keys to thinking and problem-solving.

Formal opportunities to use the SODAS method arise when an aggressive youth needs to develop a plan for the future. For example, planning for a career, employment, or college, or deciding how to develop an area of interest all lend themselves to the SODAS process.

There may be times when you will initiate a counseling session and use the SODAS process to help a youth develop a plan for more personal issues (e.g., making friends, personal hygiene, etc.). Take a future-oriented approach to these sessions, and be receptive to the youth's attempts to initiate sessions.

Problem-solving counseling has two important goals – to help aggressive youth arrive at sound solutions to their problems and to teach them how to solve problems in a systematic, rational way. The SODAS process, coupled with important quality components (e.g., empathy, listening skills, etc.) can help caregivers accomplish both goals.

Contracts

One effective way to change behavior with proactive aggressive children and adolescents is to use contracts. Basically, contracts are agreements between you and a youth that clearly spell out what the youth will earn from you when he or she behaves in certain ways. With contracts, privileges are contingent on specific behaviors you want to see from your kids. For example, you could tell a youth, "When you finish cleaning your room, you can go out and play." If you were to write down this proposal, you would make a contract.

Contracts have three main points: 1) specify the behavior the youth needs to change; 2) specify what privileges can be earned; and 3) specify how long the agreement is in effect. They can be used in a variety of situations, including:

♦ **When you want to focus on a particular aggressive behavior.** A child may frequently lose self-control, take things he or she wants from others, or yell and curse when asked to do something.

♦ **When a child has a goal in mind.** A child may want to work toward earning money for a new bike, having a later bedtime, or being allowed to go out with friends.

♦ **When you have a particular goal you'd like a youth to achieve.** You may want a youth to stop bullying younger children, decrease the amount of time he or she loses self-control, decrease the severity of aggressive behaviors, or increase the number of positive comments the youth makes about others.

In each of these situations, a contract could be used to monitor and record the progress a youth makes toward a goal.

Here's how a contract might work with Jack, a 13-year-old boy who consistently bullies other children to get things he wants from them.

Jack's Contract

I, Jack, agree not to tease or bully other kids. That means I will not yell, verbally threaten, curse, hit, or punch others. I have to do this for two weeks in a row before I earn a later bedtime on the weekends. If I do bully and tease other kids during this time, I will have to go to bed one-half hour earlier the following two weekends. This contract starts today.

We (caregivers) agree to let Jack stay up until 11:30 p.m. on Friday and Saturday nights when he doesn't bully or tease other kids for two weeks in a row. We will mark the calendar each day that Jack doesn't bully or tease other kids. This will continue for two weeks or until the contract is renegotiated.

_____   _____
(Jack's signature)   (Date)

_____
(Caregivers' signature)

Here's another example of a contract. In this situation, the caregiver and 12-year-old Frannie discussed how Frannie could help others and earn a movie rental.

Frannie's Contract

I, Frannie, will help other kids or adults at least two times each day for the next 10 days before I am able to rent a movie. This means that I will help others with their chores or homework, make positive and encouraging statements, find tasks to be done (like taking out the trash) without being asked, and help my caregivers with other tasks when they ask me without complaining or arguing. I understand that if I don't do this, I don't get to rent a movie.

We (caregivers) will let Frannie rent a movie when she completes the agreement that is discussed here. We will go over Fannie's helping behavior(s) each night. We will continue this contract for 10 days.

_____   _____
(Frannie's signature)   (Date)

_____
(Caregivers' signature)

Tips for Successful Contracts

♦ **State the goal positively.** Say "When you finish your homework, you can watch TV" instead of, "If you don't finish your homework, you won't get to watch TV." Both of these statements can be true, but it's easier to reach a goal if you're working toward something positive.

♦ **Follow through on the agreement.** Be sure to review your child's progress each day and provide encouragement to keep going. When a child reaches the goal, give what you promised. And pile on the praise!

♦ **Make the goals specific and measurable.** A goal of "completing homework each night" is easier to measure than a goal of "doing better in school." Likewise, it's easier to measure whether a child is "offering to help others once a day" than to measure whether he or she is "being more responsible." Being specific and clear helps you to know when your child has reached the goal.

♦ **Keep the goals reasonable.** Setting reachable goals is especially important when you are first introducing the idea of a contract.

♦ **Make it fun.** Using contracts to help kids reach goals and experience success is more enjoyable if it's fun for you and the child. Make a big deal out of each day's progress and use lots of praise as the child works toward the goal.

Contracts are a great way to help kids see the successes they achieve. They also open lines of communication so caregivers and children can work toward goals together. Identifying goals and planning requires conversation between the caregiver and child. For both to be winners, negotiation is necessary. The time spent setting up contracts shows kids that you care and are interested in helping them succeed.

Before kids get to do what they want, they have to keep their end of the bargain.

Contracts are simple, straightforward, and geared toward helping caregivers and children make improvements and get things accomplished.

Other-Centered Rationales

Rationales are reasons that let youth know why they should use a particular skill or behavior. Rationales are important components of all the Boys Town Teaching Interactions because youngsters are much more likely to engage in positive behavior if they understand why it is important.

When you first begin working with aggressive youth, you will likely use rationales that let them know how they will personally benefit from using a skill or behavior correctly, or what negative consequences they might receive if they do not use the skill or behavior correctly. With proactive aggressive youth, it is essential to eventually move beyond using these two kinds of rationales and begin using other-centered rationales.

Other-centered rationales focus on how a youngster's behavior affects others. Using them creates great opportunities for developing morals and positive values in youth. Research shows that one of the best ways to teach morals and positive values is by using other-centered rationales. Saying things like, "When you hit someone, it hurts them," or "When you yell and curse at me, it hurts my feelings," are easy ways to let kids know that their aggressive behavior is harmful and that they need to be sensitive to others. Even though research shows that children don't develop moral reasoning until they are about 7 years old (Piaget, 1932), they still benefit from hearing these rationales when they are very young. Frequently using other-centered rationales with proactive aggressive youth helps to create an atmosphere that teaches kids how valuable morals and high standards for behavior are. Kids must learn these important lessons in order to become respected and valued members of society.

Sample Treatment Plans

Now let's pull all this together. This section contains sample Treatment Plans for two proactive aggressive kids who are being treated in different settings. The first example takes place in a school setting; the second is in a residential group home environment. The two examples present a short summary of each youngster's behavioral and family history, and a completed Treatment Plan.

The information contained in each summary has been compiled through a comprehensive and careful evaluation process. Treatment strategies appear in bold type and specific social skills that are targeted for teaching appear in bold italic type so that you can see how they can be incorporated into a Treatment Plan.

Example 1

Robert is a 12-year-old boy who lives at home with his mother and 15-year-old brother. Robert's father is currently in jail for assaulting a police officer. On numerous occasions when he was drunk, Robert's father beat Robert and his older brother. After one particularly severe beating, Robert was hospitalized for a week for treatment of three broken ribs.

After being evaluated by a mental health professional at the school's insistence, Robert was diagnosed with Attention-Deficit/ Hyperactivity Disorder. He currently takes medication on a daily basis for this disorder. In situations that involve groups in school, Robert is easily distracted and overstimulated. He frequently does not pay attention during class activities and assignments, and repeatedly interrupts his teacher. Robert is fairly well-liked by other students, but has tremendous difficulty in his relationships with adults and in responding to their feedback or criticism. He also engages in activities without asking permission, which also results in his teachers giving feedback and correction that is difficult for him to accept. When Robert's teachers correct him for his misbehavior or tell him "No," Robert regularly becomes verbally and physically aggressive. Typically, when Robert loses self-control in school, he immediately begins to argue loudly, swear, and throw his school supplies and books. On more than one occasion, these items have hit teachers, resulting in minor injuries. Robert's teachers have reported on several occasions that they have observed Robert smirking and laughing to himself on his way to the office after a situation where he lost self-control. In addition, Robert has been overheard telling other students things like, "Teachers are afraid of me " and "I've got these stupid teachers in my hip pocket."

Finally, Robert's teachers report that he "teases and bullies" other students – especially younger or smaller kids – when they have something he wants. Recently, Robert punched a younger boy in the face, breaking the boy's glasses and injuring the boy's eye. Robert wanted the candy sale money the young boy had collected for the school's annual fund-raiser. Robert's Treatment Plan at school follows.

111

School Progress Conference Report
Summary of Social Skills from All Teachers

Student: Robert   **Grade:** 6th

Core Teacher: Mrs. Jones   **Date:** 3/1

Social Skills Summary – From All Subject Areas

Motivation System: Daily __X__   Progress _____   Merit _____

Key:

1 = Frequent Problem   2 = Occasional Problem   3 = Excellent Relations/Behavior

Adult Relations: 1   **School Rules:** 1

Peer Relations: 1   **Classroom Behaviors:** 1

Social Skill Areas of Strength: *Appropriate Voice Tone* and *Greeting Others*

Social Skill Areas in Need of Improvement: *Following Instructions, Accepting Consequences, Accepting Criticism, Accepting Adult Authority, Showing Sensitivity to Others, Following Rules, Getting the Teacher's Attention, Seeking Positive Attention, Staying on Task, Completing Tasks*

Number of Office Referrals to Date: 13

Special Program Modifications or Interventions Implemented in Past Year (e.g., behavioral **contracts**, contract for and/or placement in Achievement Plus classroom, etc.): For Robert's Attention-Deficit/Hyperactivity Disorder, we developed and agreed on a contract that stated:

1. Robert earns bonus points in the classroom for each 10-minute interval that he stays on task. He can use the points on a daily basis at the school store.

2. For completing tasks on time (e.g., a classroom task or homework assignment), Robert earns bonus points that can be used each day at the school store.

3. When Robert goes one week without an office referral, he earns bonus points for the school auction.

Student Enjoys Spending Points On: Baseball cards, gum, and posters

New Target Behaviors for Social Skill Instruction: *Accepting "No" Answers, Accepting Criticism, Following Instructions, Disagreeing Appropriately, Showing Respect, Showing Sensitivity to Others*

School
Individual Education Plan (IEP)

Student: Robert   **Grade:** 6th

Core Teacher: Mrs. Jones   **Date:** 3/1

Social Skills Assessment – (Core teachers do not fill in)

Motivation System: Daily __X__   Progress _____   Merit _____

Behaviors most often resulting in negative consequences:

Failure to follow instructions, accept criticism, accept consequences, accept adult authority, showing sensitivity to others

Behaviors most often reinforced with positive consequences:

Using appropriate voice tone, asking for help, greeting others, being on time

---

Curriculum Areas to Be Covered This: TRIMESTER   <u>SEMESTER</u>   YEAR

Introduction to basic concepts in:

1) Nature of the outdoors   2) Fossils   3) Magnetism, Electricity

4) Oceans   5) Current issues in science

Social Skills Checklist (Ratings from checklist summary)

1- Frequent Problems   2-Occasional Problems
3-Excellent relations/Behavior

ADULT RELATIONS	(1)	2	3
PEER RELATIONS	(1)	2	3
SCHOOL RULES	(1)	2	3
CLASSROOM BEHAVIORS	(1)	2	3

OTHER OBSERVATIONS: Robert regularly displays verbally and physically aggressive behaviors toward other students and teachers. Following these aggressive acts, Robert openly boasts about his negative behavior to other students. Due to his Attention-Deficit/Hyperactivity Disorder, Robert also has a difficult time concentrating on any task for longer than a few minutes. This leads to negative consequences and frustration for Robert. But in order to deal with this issue, we must first concentrate on reducing Robert's aggression.

This student will improve his/her behaviors by ____(Date)____ through emphasis on the following social skills:

Date Started   Date Ended

3/1   *Following Instructions*

3/1   *Accepting Criticism and Consequences*

3/1   *Accepting Adult Authority*

3/1   *Showing Sensitivity to Others*

Measurement Devices: Point card review, teacher observations

Adjustments in Methods, Content, Level, etc., Necessary to Meet the Individual Needs of This Student

(Tape recorder; oral tests; learning activity packets; seating; precision teaching channels – see/say, think/say, hear/say, hear/touch, hear/write, think/write, etc.; length of assignments; peer tutoring; and so on.) If none, write "none at this time."

Date Started

3/1   A **contract** will be written that states that Robert can earn bonus points after each class period in which he *follows all instructions* given by his teacher. He can use these points at the school store.

3/1   A **contract** will be written that states that Robert can earn bonus points after each class period in which he *accepts all consequences and criticism* given by his teacher. Robert can earn bonus points that can be used each day at the school store.

3/1   A **contract** will be written that states that when Robert **goes one week without an aggressive incident,** he earns bonus points for the school auction.

Rationales for above adjustments determined by observations, formal tests, informal tests, medical reports, point card review, and teacher observations.

Example 2

Marie is a 15-year-old girl who has been in four out-of-home placements in four years. Currently, she is receiving treatment in a residential group home program. Marie has a history of being sexually abused by her natural father (who later committed suicide), and also by her stepfather. At age 11, Marie became sexually active with older boys and currently displays an extremely advanced knowledge of sexual issues for her age. In social situations with adults and other kids, Marie demonstrates many pseudo-mature and overly sophisticated behaviors (e.g., too much make-up, making and laughing at sexual innuendoes and jokes, and others). In fact, Marie tends to treat adults as peers and is overly affectionate with them. Her male teachers at school have repeatedly expressed concerns about having Marie in class.

When confronted about these behaviors – as well as other problem behaviors like dishonesty, manipulation, and stealing – by her Family-Teachers in the group home, Marie becomes verbally and physically aggressive. Typically, she starts screaming and crying. But her Family-Teachers have observed that she can "turn the tears on and off like a faucet." Once Marie recognized that screaming and crying wouldn't help her to escape the consequences of her negative behaviors, she began threatening to kill herself by swallowing pills or drinking cleaning supplies. These self-harm threats have twice resulted in short stays at a locked inpatient psychiatric facility. Marie said she "hated being locked up," and didn't exhibit any aggressive or self-harm behavior while at the inpatient program. Marie's treatment team has concluded that in order to adequately help Marie with her sexual abuse issues, they must first address her aggression problem.

Treatment Plan
Group Home Program

Name: Marie   **Motivation System:** Daily   **Date:** 4/1

Diagnostic/Referral Problem: Aggression

Target Skill: #1 *Accepting Consequences*

Baseline: Percent of teaching to target skill per week = 12%

Frequency of problem behavior per week = 13 incidents

Percent of positive displayed skill per week = 15%

Problem Definition:

When given a consequence, Marie screams, curses, and begins to cry. She blames others for her behavior. Often, she becomes verbally abusive; this is more prevalent when she is not expecting a consequence (e.g., phone call from school about her negative behavior). Lately, she has begun making self-harm statements. These behaviors happen regardless of who gives the consequence or the amount of the consequence.

Long-Term Goal: Percent of teaching to target skill per week = 25%

Frequency of problem behavior per week = 0-1 incidents

Percent of positive displayed skill per week = 80%

Treatment Strategies:

Social Skill Teaching: 1) Quiz Marie on the components of *accepting consequences* two times per day; 2) **Proactive Teaching** session one time per day; 3) **Preventively prompt** before each consequence; 4) Spontaneously use **Teaching Interactions** for positive and negative behavior; 5) During Family Meeting, *accepting consequences* will be taught and reviewed a minimum of one time per week using the **SODAS** problem-solving method; 6) A **contract** will be drafted that specifically states that when Marie reduces the frequency of her problem behavior by one-half during any week, she will earn a predetermined "special."

Therapy: Marie will attend **individual therapy** with Dr. Smith once a week for one-half hour.

Medications: None at this time.

Youth	Family-Teacher	Consultant

Treatment Plan
Group Home Program

Name: Marie **Motivation System:** Daily **Date:** 4/1

Diagnostic/Referral Problem: Aggression

Target Skill: #2 *Accepting Decisions of Authority*

Baseline: Percent of teaching to target skill per week = 13%

    Frequency of problem behavior per week = 23 incidents

    Percent of positive displayed skill per week = 4%

Problem Definition:

When Marie is approached by an authority figure (e.g., parents, Family-Teachers, schoolteachers, youth managers, etc.) regarding a task to be done, a rule she broke, or an incident she was involved in, Marie frequently loses self-control. She begins by arguing; when she realizes she will not get her way, she escalates into shouting and cursing, and often becomes verbally aggressive. Lately, she has begun making self-harm statements.

Long-Term Goal: Percent of teaching to target skill per week = 25%

    Frequency of problem behavior per week = 0-1 incidents

    Percent of positive displayed skill per week = 80%

Treatment Strategies:

  Social Skill Teaching: 1) Quiz Marie on the components of *accepting adult authority* two times per day; 2) **Proactive Teaching** session one time per day; 3) **Preventively prompt** as situation demands; 4) Spontaneously use **Teaching Interactions** for positive and negative behavior; 5) During Family Meeting, *accepting adult authority* will be taught and reviewed a minimum of one time per week using the **SODAS** method of problem-solving; 6) A **contract** will be drafted that specifically states that when Marie reduces the frequency of her problem behavior by one-half during any week, she will earn a predetermined "special." 7) A **work chore** jar will be used as a consequence for the times that Marie has problems in this targeted area.

  Therapy: Marie will attend **individual therapy** with Dr. Smith once a week for one-half hour.

  Medications: None at this time.

Youth	Family-Teacher	Consultant

Treatment Plan
Group Home Program

Name: Marie   **Motivation System:** Daily   **Date:** 4/1

Diagnostic/Referral Problem: Aggression

Target Skill: #3 *Expressing Feelings Appropriately*

Baseline: Percent of teaching to target skill per week = 7%

Frequency of problem behavior per week = 19 incidents

Percent of positive displayed skill per week = 4%

Problem Definition:

When confronted with situations that frustrate or upset her, Marie often loses self-control. She expresses how she feels by arguing and yelling. Frequently, she escalates her behavior to cursing and often becomes verbally abusive and verbally aggressive. Lately, she has made statements that she is going to hurt herself.

Long-Term Goal: Percent of teaching to target skill per week = 25%

Frequency of problem behavior per week = 0-1 incidents

Percent of positive displayed skill per week = 80%

Treatment Strategies:

Social Skill Teaching: 1) Quiz Marie on the components of *expressing feelings appropriately* two times per day; 2) Proactive Teaching session one time per day; 3) **Preventively prompt** as situation demands; 4) Spontaneously use **Teaching Interactions** for positive and negative behavior; 5) During Family Meeting, *expressing feelings appropriately* will be taught and reviewed a minimum of one time per week using the **SODAS** method of problem-solving; 6) **Other-centered rationales** will be used in the Teaching Interactions; 7) One day each month Marie will participate in a **"good deed day"** with the other kids in the group home. This will involve activities like serving dinner at a homeless shelter, helping in a neighborhood cleanup, and so on.

Therapy: Marie will attend **individual therapy** with Dr. Smith once a week for one-half hour. Marie will keep a **"feelings log"** and share it with her Family-Teachers (and therapist) each night.

Medications: None at this time.

Youth	Family-Teacher	Consultant

Summary

Individualizing treatment for every youngster in your care is essential if kids are to overcome their problems. The first step to individualizing treatment is to carefully and thoroughly complete an evaluation of a youngster's problem. Once this is done, a Treatment Plan can be tailored to match the needs of each child. Proactive aggressive children and adolescents have a unique set of issues and problems that require special attention and treatment. Some strategies that have proven effective for these kids include social skill instruction, work chores, the SODAS method of problem-solving, contracts, the use of other-centered rationales, and others. The appropriate use of several of these interventions is what helps make treatment effective and successful.

CHAPTER 11
Safe Environments

Not all aggressive and violent youngsters with whom you work will respond appropriately to your teaching. Unfortunately, one of the inherent hazards of working with these kids is that some are capable of erupting in hostile and dangerous ways. As a result, there may be times when you are concerned about the safety of the child, others, and yourself. Priorities change during these situations; your primary goal becomes keeping the youngster and others out of harm's way.

Every program that works with and treats aggressive youth should have policies, procedures, and training that addresses how caregivers should deal with situations when children's behaviors pose a danger to themselves or others. In many treatment programs, caregivers are required to use more-restrictive measures, like therapeutic holds or restraint techniques, to keep the child and others safe. Anytime these types of measures are necessary, caregivers should closely follow the program's policies and procedures, use only the methods they have been trained in, and notify the appropriate individual(s) (e.g., supervisor, program administrator, etc.) following the incident.

Even though "hands-on" procedures are necessary from time to time to help ensure a safe environment, caregivers should be careful not to overuse or abuse them. Treatment programs assume considerable responsibility for the youngsters in their care. In a sense, they become the parents, teachers, and protectors for each youngster. In these roles, caregivers have considerable authority as they guide and oversee nearly every aspect of each youth's life while they are in the program. Acting *in loco parentis* (in the place of parents), caregivers must serve the best interests of each youngster in every way.

Caregivers, however, do not have unbounded authority. For example, though you take on the responsibilities of and act in the place of a parent, you do not have all of a parent's rights and options. Parents can do many things for, with, and to their own children that are legally, morally, or ethically beyond the reach of any other person or agency.

Programs that care for children are supposed to act responsibly and in the best interests of each child. But this has not always been the case. Too often, caregivers have turned to abusive practices to maintain order or to ease the burdens of operating a program. Public exposure of these abuses in the 1960s and 1970s led to changes; organizations were sued, state and federal regulations were issued, legislative bodies passed new laws, new licensing and regulatory requirements were adopted, and professional standards were defined and disseminated by various newly formed accreditation organizations.

All of this activity was designed to ensure that every child-care program would indeed act in the best interests of each child. Perhaps most importantly, children came to be seen as having rights. But because the first court case involving children's rights didn't occur until the 1960s, there still is considerable confusion over the rights of children in treatment programs. Some legal interpretations of children's rights are very expansive, while practices in some treatment programs are very restrictive.

Boys Town has examined these issues and developed a comprehensive system that respects the freedom of children, prevents their abuse, and fosters humane, effective care. Our mandate is, "As much freedom as possible; as little restriction as necessary." Boys Town is committed to providing a safe, therapeutic environment for each and every child it serves. A safe environment is free of abuse, in compliance with legal and licensing guidelines, and certified by an appropriate accreditation organization. It also allows a child to grow spiritually, emotionally, intellectually, and physically. A safe environment respects the rights of a child and employs the most positive practices in caring for and treating children.

Accreditation Organizations

An excellent vehicle for developing and ensuring the safest possible environment is voluntary certification by an accreditation body that is geared to and appropriate for a specific type of child-care program. Many of the youth rights developed at Boys Town and incorporated into the Teaching Model include those that were designed and developed by nationally known and respected accreditation organizations like the Joint Commission on Accreditation of Healthcare Organizations (JCAHO) and the Council on Accreditation (COA).

Accreditation organizations exist to help develop the highest possible national standards for the care and safety of youth in treatment, and for caregiver development and performance. Many different accreditation organizations can provide a certification process for child-care programs. Certification not only helps demonstrate that a program meets performance standards, but also can assist in efforts to gain funding. Many times, a qualification for program funding is certification by an appropriate accreditation body.

Youth Rights Components

The Boys Town Teaching Model takes a multiple-component approach to promoting safe environments. These components are:

♦ Policies and procedures

♦ Training in positive interaction styles

♦ Ongoing program evaluation

♦ Regular youth interviews

♦ Feedback from outside consumers

♦ Staff Practice Inquiries

♦ Training in the rights of children

All of these components are integrated into a system of care where the main provision is safe, humane care and treatment. Information gathered through these various components is constantly used to update and modify the program, as necessary.

Policies and Procedures

The commitment to provide safe environments begins here. All caregivers are made aware of written policies and procedures that relate to protecting the rights of children. These not only emphasize the intent of the program, but also spell out the procedures that are followed when possible violations are suspected or occur. Policies and procedures set in to motion other specific components.

Training in Positive Interaction Styles

All caregivers are trained in how to interact positively with children and how to help them change their behavior while respecting their basic dignity and freedom. Also, all caregivers learn how to develop positive relationships with each child.

Ongoing Program Evaluation

Regular evaluation reports provide caregivers with systematic feedback on program effectiveness. These reports give caregivers insight into the quality of care provided for children. One of the features of a humane program is how well it succeeds in reaching the goals for which it was established. Routinely monitoring and reporting on progress helps a program achieve these goals.

Regular Youth Interviews

In addition to routine interviews during treatment, youth also are interviewed before they leave a program. During these interviews, each youngster is asked whether he or she was mistreated by caregivers or others. Youth also are asked to express their opinions about the pleasantness and support of caregivers and others, and the overall effectiveness of the program.

These questions provide important information about the treatment atmosphere, how goals are reached, and what methods are used. Such information can be used to improve caregiver interaction and communication skills, when necessary.

Feedback from Outside Consumers

Interested, involved persons from outside the program (probation officers, caseworkers, or family members) are another important source of information about the quality of care provided for troubled kids. These "consumers" are asked to assess the quality of care immediately following a youngster's departure. Their impartial impressions of the care and treatment children receive supply valuable feedback.

Staff Practice Inquiries

Any questionable practice by a caregiver is subject to a Staff Practice Inquiry. This inquiry is an investigation into a suspected violation that stems from a youth report, a consumer report, or observation by a staff member.

All allegations concerning less-than-optimal care obtained from any source are investigated thoroughly and promptly. The fact that Staff Practice Inquiries are begun quickly makes it clear that Boys Town takes its protective role seriously. All claims, regardless of their perceived validity or their perceived seriousness, are investigated in order to sensitize all caregivers to the importance of maintaining high-quality standards of care.

It is the collective responsibility of all staff members to safeguard the rights of children. Any suspected abuse observed by children, staff, or persons outside the program or facility is to be reported immediately to the appropriate supervisor, program administrator, etc., who immediately starts a Staff Practice Inquiry. The child and adult who were allegedly involved are interviewed, along with others who may have relevant information. Facts are established and conclusions are reached as quickly as possible. Quick action is important so that a situation in which a child is in danger or is uncomfortable can be rectified. It's also important to act quickly so that any potential harm to a caregiver's reputation can be minimized in situations where allegations are unfounded or untrue.

The greatest degree of confidentiality possible is maintained in all Staff Practice Inquiries. Total anonymity of the parties involved often can be maintained. This anonymity cannot be guaranteed when a child may be at some risk or when relevant persons need some information during the course of the inquiry process. For instance, parents or legal guardians are immediately informed of any allegation. In cases where serious allegations are made, child protective service agencies are informed so that they can decide whether or not to conduct their own investigation.

Another important part of Staff Practice Inquiries is the debriefing phase. Verbal and/or written reports are given to persons who have the "right to know" about any outcomes. It is important that relevant persons are kept informed, not only to protect the interests of the child, but also to protect the reputation of any innocent caregivers who are involved.

Training in the Rights of Children

Before beginning their work with children, all Boys Town caregivers receive extensive training in the rights of children. Once they begin providing treatment, caregivers are kept up to date on new developments and rights' issues through a consultant advisory process, and materials and meetings provided by supervisors. Caregivers also are required to learn and follow a set of rules and guidelines that cover youth rights. These will be explained in the next section.

Rights: Rules and Guidelines

The remainder of this chapter outlines and explains 15 specific youth rights. These are not all inclusive but give a good overview of the elements that are important in ensuring the safety of youth who are in the Boys Town program.

In each of these areas, there are rules and guidelines. **Rules** are empirical generaliza-

tions, or "rules of thumb." Certain priorities are called "rules" because they are not meant to be modified. In the very rare circumstances when this happens, changes never occur without advance permission from a program supervisor. **Guidelines** are less-explicit generalizations that serve as guiding principles around which caregivers must exercise discretion and sound judgment, depending upon a youngster's needs and the circumstances of a situation. Guidelines are considered to be prudent practices in typical situations.

1. Informed Consent

Youth and their parents or legal guardians should be included in the decision-making process and informed of all aspects of proposed treatments and program components. Ideally, this information is shared before the youth is admitted to the program.

Rules:

♦ Informed consent is a process where youth and their parents or legal guardians are given a clear, concise explanation of the youth's condition (if fully diagnosed); proposed interventions, treatments, or medications; potential benefits, risks, and side effects of proposed interventions, treatments, or medications; problems related to recovery (if applicable); likelihood of success; any alternative medications, treatments, or interventions; and the youth's right, to the extent permitted by law, to refuse medications, treatments, or interventions.

Guidelines:

♦ At the time of intake or during a youth's first visit, a caregiver reviews the program goals and specific expectations regarding the youth's informed consent to participate in the program. Included is a description of how caregivers will ask the youth to confirm his or her willingness to participate in treatment throughout his or her stay and how this will be documented by caregivers. At the end of the initial interview, the youth receives a written informed consent document that contains all the information that was described to the youth. The youth and his or her parents or legal guardians sign the document, as does the caregiver who described the program and its expectations. Basically, the youth enters into a consensual "behavioral contract" with the program. This upfront Proactive Teaching helps increase the chance for cooperative participation from the youth (and family), and enhances the chance for successful treatment.

2. Right to Nourishment

Caregivers must provide each child with healthy food and proper nutrition. A major right of each child is the right to healthy nourishment.

Rules:

♦ Caregivers must provide three nutritionally adequate meals to each youth each and every day.

♦ The three main meals (e.g., breakfast, lunch, and supper) should never be used as a consequence or sold as a privilege. A child has a right to these because he or she is a person.

♦ Meals should never intentionally be made less adequate, less tasty, or less nutritious for any reason.

♦ Medical advice and guardian consent should be obtained before initiating weight-loss programs.

Guidelines:

♦ Caregivers should provide a wide variety of nutritious foods for children, including ethnic preferences.

♦ Caregivers should avoid imposing their own personal food preferences (e.g., vegetarian or sugar-free diets) or fad diets (e.g., eggs and grapefruit for each meal) on children.

♦ Nutritious snacks such as fruits or vegetables are best made freely available.

♦ "Junk food" (e.g., chips, candy bars, etc.) should be available only in moderation. Prohibiting "junk food," however, usually is unreasonable and unenforceable.

♦ Caregivers should be able to provide documentation of adequate nutrition (e.g., keep menus that have been approved by a licensed dietitian for six months).

3. Right to Communicate with Significant Others

Caregivers should actively teach children how to communicate with others. Healthy relationships with significant others are desirable for all children.

Rules:

♦ Children have a right to seek advocacy or communicate with significant others like parents, guardians, probation officers, or clergy.

♦ Communication with significant others should not be used as a consequence or sold as a privilege (e.g., because Johnny did not apologize to a caregiver, he cannot call his mother).

♦ Caregivers should provide methods (i.e., mail or phone) for routine and emergency contact with significant others.

♦ Caregivers should advocate for each child's right to present his or her own case directly to any authority in any formal or informal proceedings.

Guidelines:

♦ Caregivers can exercise reasonable control over the form (e.g., two long-distance calls per week) and timing (e.g., allow a call to probation officer when child is calm) of communication.

♦ Control over the form, frequency, or timing of communication should not be unreasonable (e.g., even though a child is not perfectly calm, he or she can call a guardian after reasonable attempts have been made to calm the child; thus, after three hours of discussion, it would be prudent to let the child call).

4. Right to Respect of Body and Person

Caregivers should use interaction styles that are the most pleasant and that demonstrate humane, professional, and concerned care at all times. Physical intervention should be used only after attempts to verbally calm the youth have proven ineffective and the youth is endangering himself or herself, or others. Violence is always forbidden.

Rules:

♦ Corporal punishment is never used to discipline youngsters (e.g., never use spanking or physical exercise as a consequence).

♦ Caregivers should use restraint as a last option and only when it is necessary to prevent a child from harming himself/herself or others.

♦ Caregivers should avoid sarcasm, labeling, or name-calling that might humiliate a child (e.g., discussing John's bed-wetting in front of other kids).

♦ The use of curse words directed toward children is never appropriate.

Guidelines:

♦ Restraint is most successful (i.e., prevents injury) when the adult has physical

superiority and has been trained in restraint procedures.

♦ The least possible force should be employed when restraint is required.

5. Right to Have One's Own Possessions

Each child has a right to possessions that are commensurate with his or her developmental level and living situation. Caregivers should respect a youth's right to possessions and create a therapeutic atmosphere that facilitates children owning personal possessions.

Rules:

♦ Caregivers should ensure that children do not possess dangerous items (e.g., drugs, guns, knives, and so on).

♦ Caregivers should ensure that each child has the necessary "tools" or supplies needed for participation in therapy, school, ect., and that he or she has materials similar to those of his or her peers (e.g., books, clothes, bedding, and so on).

♦ Caregivers should never confiscate a child's possessions (other than dangerous possessions) without having the child waive his or her right to the possession or without the intent to transfer physical custody of the possession to the child's guardian.

Guidelines:

♦ Caregivers can exercise reasonable control over the possessions a youngster brings to a program (e.g., no contraband).

♦ Caregivers can limit the use of personal possessions to reasonable times or places (e.g., no radios played after lights out).

♦ If a child is restricted from appropriate use of a personal possession, he or she should be told how to earn its use back.

6. Right to Privacy

Under the right to privacy, caregivers should ensure that each child has the rights typically afforded people in our society. Each child should have personal living and storage areas. Each child's right to physical privacy should be protected.

Rules:

♦ Caregivers should not open a child's mail or listen in on phone conversations without the child's permission.

♦ Caregivers shouldn't routinely or secretly search a child's room or belongings.

♦ Caregivers should not search a youngster's person.

♦ Caregivers can release program records only to a child's legal guardian or a person who has written permission from the child's legal guardian.

Guidelines:

♦ Caregivers should ensure privacy for each child and his or her belongings (e.g., bed, dresser, clothes, and so on) in the child's living space.

♦ Public searches (e.g., announced, with the child and one other adult present) for contraband may take place when there is probable cause to search.

♦ While caregivers should not open and read youth mail, a child can be asked to open mail in front of a caregiver when there is probable cause (e.g., suspicion of a child receiving drugs from a friend).

7. Right to Freedom of Movement

Each youth has a right to a wide range of experiences commensurate with his or her age and maturity level. Procedures that physically restrict movement or consequences that pre-

vent exposure to healthy activities for extended periods of time are generally discouraged.

Rules:

♦ Seclusion procedures should be used only with a doctor's order (e.g., youth locked in a specifically designed room until the crisis is effectively resolved).

♦ Time-Out should be used only after verbal teaching interventions have proven temporarily ineffective. Teaching to the ongoing or antecedent behavior should take place following the Time-Out.

♦ A child should always be provided with options for earning privileges (e.g., privileges can be earned on a more-restrictive Motivation System level).

Guidelines:

♦ Caregivers can limit a youngster's movements to a given area and time (e.g., in school from 8 a.m. to 3:15 p.m.).

8. Right to Be Given Meaningful Work

Caregivers should ensure that each youth lives in a learning environment where chores, tasks, treatment goals, and privileges are meaningful experiences that enrich a child's body and mind. Ideally, consequences for problem behaviors should have an immediate teaching benefit and should not be principally punishing in nature.

Rules:

♦ Caregivers should never give "make work" tasks (e.g., cleaning a floor with a toothbrush, digging a hole and refilling it, or writing a sentence 500 times).

♦ Procedures that are designed solely to punish should not be employed (e.g., making a youth kneel and hold a broom above his or her head, or making a youth eat a catsup sandwich for squirting catsup on someone).

Guidelines:

♦ Caregivers can assign chores and tasks related to daily living that teach family or personal values (e.g., making one's bed or cleaning one's room).

♦ Removing a youth from typical adolescent responsibilities or activities should not be a consequence for problem behaviors. Note: While a youth sometimes must be removed from activities, this should be done only when the behavior is so serious that it negates the benefit of continued participation. The youth can resume participation when the behavior improves.

9. Right to File Material

Caregivers should make provisions for letting children know what is being communicated in treatment reports. Written documentation should be consistent with daily treatment strategies and target areas. Good child care ensures that the child knows his or her treatment goals and progress.

Rules:

♦ Caregivers should not deny a child the right to know what they are writing in treatment reports.

♦ A caregiver should be present whenever a child is reviewing file material.

♦ Caregivers must ensure that all file material is secure and stored in a locked cabinet when they are not present to provide supervision.

Guidelines:

♦ Caregivers should routinely have youth sign treatment reports.

♦ Sensitive file materials (e.g., psychological evaluations or social histories) should be stored in a locked file cabinet. This makes it less likely that a child will be exposed to confusing or emotionally laden material.

10. Right to Interact with Others

Youth should be taught skills that enhance their relationships with peers and adults. Youth should be provided with ample opportunities to interact with peers of the same and opposite sex. Interacting with people is a basic right. Caregivers should monitor each youngster's social contacts to ensure that they are appropriate.

Rules:

♦ Isolation should not be used as a consequence for problem behaviors (e.g., instructing other children not to talk to a child as a consequence for a problem behavior).

Guidelines:

♦ Caregivers may limit interactions between children and some peers (e.g., children with known substance abuse or sexual development problems may be limited in their interactions with peers with similar problems).

♦ Caregivers may limit when and how children interact with peers (e.g., no telephone contacts on weeknights after 9:30).

♦ Caregivers may ask other youth to leave the area when they are working with a particular youth, such as in a Crisis Teaching situation.

11. Right to Goals and Privileges

Commensurate with his or her age and development, each child should at all times have a Treatment Plan that provides the opportunity to work toward desired goals or privileges. All Motivation Systems should afford the youth an opportunity to earn some privileges. In addition to having a Treatment Plan, each child should know the specific behaviors that are needed to fulfill it.

Rules:

♦ No child should be given consequences that prohibit him or her from earning any privileges for unreasonably long periods of time (e.g., more than 24 hours).

♦ Children should have the opportunity to earn at least basics, snacks, TV, and one phone call every 24 hours.

♦ Children should not be given consequences without being told how they can remove the consequences and regain their privileges.

Guidelines:

♦ Caregivers should extend special advocacy for children who have not earned privileges for two days in succession (e.g., spend more time encouraging and interacting with a child).

12. Right to Basic Clothing Necessities

Children should be provided with appropriate dress and leisure clothing commensurate with their age and sex. Caregivers should ensure that each child's basic clothing needs are met at all times.

Rules:

♦ Basic clothing needs should never be limited as a consequence for a problem behavior (e.g., child wears no shoes as a consequence for losing them, or a child is forced to wear inadequate or inappropriate clothing as a consequence).

Guidelines:

♦ A child's personal preference in clothing should be strongly considered by caregivers so long as the personal preference is not extremely deviant in style or price (e.g., neither "punk" styles nor designer quality need to be provided).

♦ Caregivers can limit the style of clothing so that it is consistent with the treatment goals of an individual youth (e.g., a child should not wear sexually provocative clothing, gang-related clothing, or clothing that contains material that is profane or related to drugs, alcohol, or cigarettes).

13. Right to the Natural Elements

Each child has a right to natural elements such as fresh air, light, sunshine, and outdoor exercise. Healthy outdoor activities should be a routine part of every child's experience. Caregivers should ensure that each child has the opportunity to experience the natural elements each day.

Rules:

♦ Neither the natural elements nor indoor light should be used as a consequence (e.g., a child should be able to get some outside exercise even when on a restricted Motivation System).

Guidelines:

♦ Each child should be provided with the opportunity for outside activities each day (e.g., walking or playing in a secured outside area).

♦ Caregivers can regulate the amount of time spent outside and the degree of supervision provided for each child.

14. Right to One's Own Bed

Each youth has a right to a personal bed and a private sleeping area.

Rule:

♦ A child's access to a personal bed or bedding should never be restricted during normal sleeping hours.

Guidelines:

♦ Caregivers may have more than one youngster sharing a bedroom if ample space and privacy is provided.

♦ Caregivers may regulate a youngster's access to his or her bedroom during nonsleeping hours or limit privacy of the sleeping area when a child is at-risk (e.g., when a child is suicidal).

15. Right to Leave the Program

Caregivers must ensure that a child is provided care in accordance with the reasonable wishes of the legal guardian. Children have the right to advocacy by their guardian. This includes the guardian's right to place a child in or remove a child from a program.

Rules:

♦ Caregivers cannot prohibit a child from returning home or going to another less-restrictive placement upon the request of his or her legal guardian.

Guidelines:

♦ Caregivers may provide advocacy for a child staying at a treatment program in the form of rationales and by acting promptly on a parent's or guardian's request to remove the child.

♦ Caregivers should not impede the orderly transition of a child from a treatment program to his or her next placement.

Summary

When working with and caring for aggressive and violent youth, there will be times when they don't respond to your teaching, and the safety of others and the child will become your paramount concern. During these times, you should implement the policies and procedures that are in place, and use only the methods that you have been trained in.

At the same time, however, caregivers also should be very concerned about protecting and ensuring the rights and privileges of children. The rules, guidelines, and processes described in this chapter promote and foster this concern. Success in ensuring children's rights is not brought about by procedures alone; there also must be a "sense of quality" instilled in each caregiver. Each caregiver must understand that it is his or her competence in carrying out Treatment Plans and diligence in monitoring his or her own actions and the actions of others that makes the real difference. Rules, guidelines, and procedures are necessary, but it is the commitment to provide the highest quality care possible that ensures a safe environment for each child.

APPENDIX

Social Skills for Aggressive Youth

The charts in this Appendix list social skills that can be taught as part of treatment for kids who tend to use either reactive aggressive behaviors or proactive aggressive behaviors. (For complete step-by-step breakdowns of these skills, please refer to *Teaching Social Skills to Youth*, Dowd & Tierney, 1992.) There are two charts; one is labeled "Social Skills for Proactive Aggression" and the other is labeled "Social Skills for Reactive Aggression." As we've discussed throughout this book, once a caregiver evaluates and determines the type of aggressive behavior a child tends to display, he or she is better equipped to develop an effective, therapeutic, and successful Treatment Plan and to identify the social skills that will help the child move toward prosocial, appropriate behaviors.

The two charts are intended to be a resource and a guide for caregivers who are in the process of selecting and assigning appropriate social skills for teaching. Many of the social skills included in each chart overlap and can be used with proactive aggressive kids

or reactive aggressive kids. However, many skills pertain specifically to behaviors typically exhibited by one type of youth or the other. (Keep in mind that once you assess and diagnose a child's problem as either proactive or reactive aggression, and begin to utilize social skill instruction as a treatment strategy, any skill that needs to be taught should be taught, regardless of what chart it is in.)

In the charts, skills are classified as basic, intermediate, advanced, or complex. Generally speaking, when caregivers first begin working with an aggressive youngster, the youth will need to learn the basic skills first. The basic skills are necessary building blocks; they provide a foundation for the other higher-level skills. Mastery of the basic skills improves the child's chances for successfully learning intermediate, advanced, and complex skills.

Social Skills for Proactive Aggression

Basic Skills Group

Accepting Consequences

Accepting Criticism

Accepting "No" Answers

Disagreeing Appropriately

Following Instructions

Showing Respect

Showing Sensitivity to Others

Talking to Others

Intermediate Skills Group

Accepting Apologies from Others

Accepting Compliments

Accepting Decisions of Authority

Appropriate Voice Tone

Appropriate Word Choice

Asking for Clarification

Checking In (or Checking Back)

Complying with Reasonable Requests

Following Rules

Getting Another Person's Attention

Getting the Teacher's Attention

Giving Compliments

Interrupting Appropriately

Listening to Others

Making a Request (Asking a Favor)

Making an Apology

Offering Assistance or Help

Participating in Activities

Positive Statements about Others

Saying "No" Assertively

Showing Appreciation

Showing Interest

Structured Problem-Solving (SODAS)

Volunteering

Waiting Your Turn

Advanced Skills Group

Accepting Defeat or Loss

Accepting Help or Assistance

Accepting Winning Appropriately

Analyzing Skills Needed for Different Situations

Analyzing Social Situations

Borrowing from Others

Care of Others' Property

Compromising with Others

Choosing Appropriate Friends

Communicating Honestly

Controlling Sexually Abusive Impulses toward Others

Controlling the Impulse to Lie

Controlling the Impulse to Steal

Cooperating with Others

Coping with Anger and Aggression from Others

Dealing with Accusation

Dealing with Boredom

Dealing with Contradictory Messages

Dealing with Embarrassing Situations

Dealing with Failure

Dealing with Frustration

132

Dealing with Group Pressure

Dealing with Rejection

Decision-Making

Delaying Gratification

Expressing Feelings Appropriately

Giving Instructions

Giving Rationales

Interacting Appropriately with Members of the Opposite Sex

Keeping Property in Its Place

Making New Friends

Making Restitution (Compensating)

Negotiating with Others

Persevering on Tasks and Projects

Preparing for a Stressful Conversation

Preventing Trouble with Others

Problem-Solving a Disagreement

Relaxation Strategies

Responding to Complaints

Responding to Others' Feelings

Responding to Teasing

Self-Correcting Own Behaviors

Self-Reporting Own Behaviors

Self-Talk or Instruction

Setting Appropriate Boundaries

Spontaneous Problem-Solving

Sportsmanship

Use of Appropriate Humor

Use of Appropriate Language

Complex Skills Group

Altering One's Environment

Asking for Advice

Assertiveness

Assessing Own Abilities

Conflict Resolution

Displaying Appropriate Control

Expressing Empathy and Understanding for Others

Formulating Strategies

Gathering Information

Goal-Setting

Laughing at Oneself

Maintaining Relationships

Making an Appropriate Complaint

Moral and Spiritual Decision-Making

Patience

Planning Ahead

Recognizing Moods of Others

Self-Monitoring and Reflection

Thought-Stopping

Tolerating Differences

Social Skills for Reactive Aggression

Basic Skills Group

Accepting Consequences

Accepting Criticism

Accepting "No" Answers

Following Instructions

Disagreeing Appropriately

Talking to Others

Intermediate Skills Group

Accepting Compliments

Accepting Decisions of Authority

Anger Control Strategies

Asking for Clarification

Asking for Help

Correcting Another Person
(or Giving Criticism)

Following Rules

Getting Another Person's Attention

Getting the Teacher's Attention

Ignoring Distractions by Others

Listening to Others

Making a Request (Asking a Favor)

Making an Apology

Positive Self-Statements

Reporting Other Youths' Behavior
(or Peer Reporting)

Resisting Peer Pressure

Saying "No" Assertively

Seeking Positive Attention

Structured Problem-Solving (SODAS)

Waiting Your Turn

Advanced Skills Group

Accepting Defeat or Loss

Analyzing Skills Needed for
Different Situations

Analyzing Social Situations

Choosing Appropriate Friends

Controlling Emotions

Cooperating with Others

Coping with Anger and Aggression
from Others

Coping with Change

Coping with Conflict

Coping with Sad Feelings (or Depression)

Dealing with an Accusation

Dealing with Being Left Out

Dealing with Contradictory Messages

Dealing with Embarrassing Situations

Dealing with Failure

Dealing with Fear

Dealing with Frustration

Dealing with Group Pressure

Dealing with Rejection

Decision-Making

Delaying Gratification

Expressing Appropriate Affection

Expressing Feelings Appropriately

Expressing Pride in Accomplishments

Making New Friends

Making Restitution (Compensating)

Negotiating with Others

Persevering on Tasks and Projects

Preparing for a Stressful Conversation

Preventing Trouble with Others

Problem-Solving a Disagreement

Relaxation Strategies

Responding to Complaints

Responding to Others' Feelings

Responding to Teasing

Self-Advocacy

Self-Correcting Own Behaviors

Self-Talk or Instruction

Setting Appropriate Boundaries

Sharing Attention with Others

Spontaneous Problem-Solving

Sportsmanship

Use of Appropriate Language

Rewarding Yourself

Self-Monitoring and Reflection

Thought-Stopping

Complex Skills Group

Accepting Self

Altering One's Environment

Asking for Advice

Assertiveness

Assessing Own Abilities

Conflict Resolution

Displaying Appropriate Control

Expressing Grief

Formulating Strategies

Gathering Information

Goal-Setting

Identifying Own Feelings

Laughing at Oneself

Maintaining Relationships

Moral and Spiritual Decision-Making

Patience

Planning Ahead

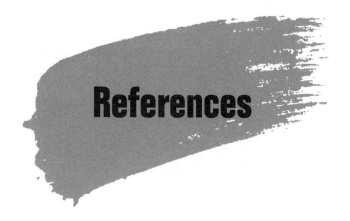

References

Ackerson, L. (1931). **Children's behavior problems** (Vol. 1). Chicago: University of Chicago Press.

Bedlington, M.M., Solnick, J.R., Braukmann, C.J., Kirigin, K.A., & Wolf, M.M. (1979, August). The correlation between some parenting behaviors, delinquency and youth satisfaction in Teaching-Family group homes. In J.R. Solnick (Chair), **Family interaction and deviant behavior.** Symposium conducted at the 87th Annual Convention of the American Psychological Association, New York.

Behar, D., & Stewart, M.A. (1982). Aggressive conduct disorder in children. **Acta Psychiatric Scandinavia, 65,** 210-220.

Braukmann, C.J., Kirigin, K.A., & Wolf, M.M. (1976). **Achievement place: The researcher's perspective.** Paper presented at the 84th Annual Convention of the American Psychological Association, Washington, DC.

Brown, G.L., Ebert, M.H., Goyer, P.F., Jimerson, D.C., Klein, W.J., Bunney, W.E., & Goodwin, F.K. (1982). Aggression, suicide and serotonin: Relationships to CSF amine metabolites. **American Journal of Psychiatry, 139,** 741-745.

Butts, J.A., Snyder, H.N., Finnegan, T.A., Augenbaugh, A.L., & Poole, R.S. (1996). **Juvenile court statistics 1994.** Washington, DC: Office of Juvenile Justice and Delinquency Prevention, U.S. Department of Justice.

Cadoret, R.J. (1978). Psychopathology in adopted-away offspring of biological parents with antisocial behavior. **Archives of General Psychiatry, 35,** 176-184.

Christiansen, K.O. (1974). Seriousness of criminality and concordance among Danish twins. In R. Hood (Ed.), **Crime, criminology and public policy** (pp. 63-67). London: Heinemann.

Cloninger, C.R., Reich, T., & Guze, S.B. (1978). Genetic-environmental interactions and antisocial behaviour. In R.D. Hare & D. Schalling (Eds.), **Psychopathic behaviour: Approaches to research** (pp. 225-237). Chichester, England: John Wiley & Sons.

Combs, M.L., & Slaby, D.A. (1977). Social skills training with children. In B.B. Lahey & A.E. Kazdin (Eds.), **Advances in clinical child psychology** (pp. 161-201). New York: Plenum Press.

Crow, R. (1974). An adoption study of antisocial personality. **Archives of General Psychiatry, 31**, 785-791.

Dishion, T.J., Loeber, R., Stouthamer-Loeber, M., & Patterson, G.R. (1984). Skill deficits and male adolescent delinquency. **Journal of Abnormal Child Psychology**, **12**, 37-54.

Dodge, K.A. (1991). The structure and function of reactive and proactive aggression. In D.J. Pepler and K.H. Rubin (Eds.), **The development and treatment of childhood aggression** (pp. 201-218). Hillsdale, NJ: Lawrence Erlbaum Associates, Inc.

Dowd, T., & Tierney, J. (1992). **Teaching social skills to youth: A curriculum for child-care providers.** Boys Town, NE: Boys Town Press.

Edelbrock, C. (1983). **The antecedents of antisocial behavior: A cross-sectional analysis.** Unpublished manuscript, University of Pittsburgh School of Medicine.

Farrington, D.P. (1978). The family background of aggressive youths. In L.A. Hersov, M. Berger, & D. Schaffer (Eds.), **Aggressive and antisocial behavior in childhood and adolescence** (pp. 73-94). Oxford, England: Pergamon Press.

Federal Bureau of Investigation. (1996). **Crime in the United States 1995.** Washington, DC: Government Printing Office.

Forgatch, D.P. (1988, February). **A social learning approach to family therapy.** Paper presented at the Taboroff Child and Adolescent Psychiatry Conference on Conduct Disorders in Children and Adolescents, Snowbird, UT.

Freedman, B.J., Rosenthal, L., Donahue, L.P. Jr., Schlundt, D.G., & McFall, R.M. (1978). A social-behavioral analysis of skill deficits in delinquent and nondelinquent adolescent boys. **Journal of Consulting and Clinical Psychology**, **46**, 1448-1462.

Friman, P.C., Handwerk, M.L., Smith, G., Larzelere, R., Lucas, C.P., & Shaffer, D. (1998). **Clinical validity of the Diagnostic Interview Schedule for Children-Child (DISC:C): Determined conduct and oppositional defiant disorders.** Manuscript submitted to the **Psychological Assessment.**

Gilbert, G.M. (1957). A survey of "referral problems" in metropolitan child guidance centers. **Journal of Clinical Psychology, 13**, 37-42.

Glueck, S., & Glueck, E.T. (1950). **Unravelling juvenile delinquency.** Cambridge, MA: Harvard University Press.

Glueck, S., & Glueck, E.T. (1968). **Delinquents and nondelinquents in perspective.** Cambridge, MA: Harvard University Press.

Goldstein, A.P., & Keller, H. (1989). **Aggressive behavior: Assessment and intervention.** New York: Pergamon.

Goldstein, A.P., Sprafkin, R.R., Gershaw, N.J., & Klien, P. (1980). **Skillstreaming the adolescent: A structured learning approach to teaching prosocial skills.** Champaign, IL: Research Press.

Grisso, T. (1996). Introduction: An interdisciplinary approach to understanding aggressive behavior in children. In C.F. Ferris & T. Grisso (Eds.), **Understanding aggressive behavior in children.** New York: The New York Academy of Sciences.

Hardy, R. (1988). **Behavior analysis: A computer-based tutorial** (computer program). DePere, WI: St. Norbert College.

Hetherington, E.M., & Martin, B. (1979). Family interaction. In H.C. Quay & J.S. Werry (Eds.), **Psychopathological disorders of childhood** (2nd ed.) (pp. 247-302). New York: John Wiley & Sons.

Hirschi, T. (1969). **Causes of delinquency.** Berkeley: University of California Press.

Hirschi, T., & Hindeland, M.J. (1977). Intelligence and delinquency: A revisionist's review. **American Sociological Review, 42**, 571-587.

Kanfer, F.H., & Saslow, S. (1969). Behavioral diagnosis. In C.M. Franks (Ed.), **Behavior therapy: Appraisal and status** (pp. 417-444). New York: McGraw-Hill.

Kazdin, A.E. (1985). **Treatment of antisocial behavior in children and adolescents.** Homewood, IL: The Dorsey Press.

Kazdin, A.E. (1987). Treatment of antisocial behavior in children: Current status and future directions. **Psychological Bulletin, 102**, 187-203.

Klein, N.C., Alexander, J.F., & Parsons, B.Y. (1977). Impact of family system interventions on recidivism and sibling delinquency: A model of primary prevention and program evaluation. **Journal of Consulting and Clinical Psychology, 45,** 469-474.

Lange, A.J., & Jakubowski, P. (1976). **Responsible assertive behavior: Cognitive/behavioral procedures for trainers.** Champaign, IL: Research Press.

Ledingham, J.E., & Schwartzman, A.E. (1984). A 3-year follow-up of aggressive and withdrawn behavior in childhood: Preliminary findings. **Journal of Abnormal Child Psychology, 12,** 157-168.

Lesser, G.S. (1959). The relationships between various forms of aggression and popularity among lower-class children. **Journal of Educational Psychology, 50,** 20-25.

Loeber, R., & Hay, D. (1997). Key issues in the development of aggression and violence from childhood to early adulthood. **Annual Review in Psychology, 48,** 371-410.

MacFarlane, J.W., Allen, L., & Honzik, M.P. (1954). **A developmental study of the behavior problems of normal children 21 months and 14 years.** Berkeley: University of California Press.

Maerov, S.L., Brummett, B., Patterson, G.R., & Reid, J.B. (1978). Coding of family interactions. In J.B. Reid (Ed.), **A social learning approach to family intervention** (pp. 21-37). Eugene, OR: Castalia.

Mattsson, A., Schalling, D., Olweus, D., Low, H., & Svensson, J. (1980). Plasma testosterone, aggressive behavior, and personality dimensions in young male delinquents. **Journal of the American Academy of Child Psychiatry, 19,** 476-490.

McCord, W., McCord, J., & Zola, J.K. (1959). **Origins of crime.** New York: Columbia University Press.

Mednick, S.A. (1978). You don't need a weatherman! In L. Otten (Ed.), **Colloquim on the correlates of crime and the determinants of criminal behavior** (pp. 133-151). Arlington, VA: MITRE.

Mednick, S.A., & Hutchings, B. (1978). Genetic and psychophysiological factors in asocial behaviour. In R.D. Hare & D. Schalling (Eds.), **Psychopathic behaviour: Approaches to research** (pp. 239-253). Chichester, England: John Wiley & Sons.

Nye, F.I. (1958). **Family relationships and delinquent behavior.** New York: John Wiley & Sons.

Olweus, D. (1996). Bullying at school: Knowledge base and an effective intervention program. In C.F. Ferris & T. Grisso (Eds.), **Understanding aggressive behavior in children** (pp. 265-276). New York: The New York Academy of Sciences.

Patterson, G.R. (1971). **Applications of social learning to family life.** Champaign, IL: Research Press.

Patterson, G.R. (1982). **Coercive family process.** Eugene, OR: Castalia.

Patterson, G.R. (Ed.) (1990). **Depression and aggression in family interaction.** Hillsdale, NJ: Erlbaum.

Patterson, G.R., DeBaryshe, B.D., & Ramsey, E. (1989). A developmental perspective on antisocial behavior. **American Psychologist,** February, 329-335.

Patterson, G.R., Dishion, T.J., & Bank, L. (1984). Family interaction: A process model of deviancy training. **Aggressive Behavior, 10**, 253-267.

Patterson, G.R., Dishion, T.J., & Reid, J.B. (1989). **A social learning approach: Volume 4, a coercion model.** Eugene, OR: Castalia.

Patterson, G.R., & Forgatch, M. (1987). **Parents and adolescents: 1. Living together.** Eugene, OR: Castalia.

Patterson, G.R., Forgatch, M.S., Yoerger, K., & Stoolmiller, M. (1998). Variables that initiate and maintain an early-onset trajectory for juvenile offending. **Development and Psychopathology, 10,** 531-547.

Patterson, G.R., & Stouthamer-Loeber, M. (1984). The correlation of family management practices and delinquency. **Child Development, 55,** 1299-1307.

Peter, V.J. (1999). **What makes Boys Town successful.** Boys Town, NE: Boys Town Press.

Piaget, J. (1932). **The moral judgment of the child.** New York: Harcourt Brace Jovanovich.

Raz, E. (1977). **The relationship of youth ratings and future delinquent behavior.** Unpublished master's thesis. Lawrence, KS: University of Kansas.

Reiss, A.J., & Roth, J.A. (Eds.). (1993). **Understanding and preventing violence.** Washington, DC: National Academy Press.

Robins, L.N. (1966). **Deviant children grown up.** Baltimore: Williams & Wilkins.

Robins, L.N. (1978). Sturdy childhood predictors of adult antisocial behavior: Replications from longitudinal studies. **Psychological Medicine, 8,** 611-622.

Roosa, J.B. (1973). **SOCS: Situations, options, consequences, simulation: A technique for teaching social interactions.** Unpublished paper presented to the American Psychological Association, Montreal.

Rutter, M., & Giller, H. (1983). **Juvenile delinquency: Trends and perspectives.** New York: Penguin Books.

Rutter, M., Tizard, J., & Whitmore, K. (Eds.) (1970). **Education, health and behavior.** London: Longmans.

Sheard, M.H. (1975). Lithium in the treatment of aggression. **Journal of Nervous and Mental Disease**, **160**, 108-118.

Sickmund, M., Snyder, H.N., & Poe-Yamagata, E. (1997). **Juvenile offenders and victims: 1997 update on violence.** Washington, DC: Office of Juvenile Justice and Delinquency Prevention.

Snyder, J., Dishion, T.J., & Patterson, G.R. (1986). Determinants and consequences of associating with deviant peers during preadolescence and adolescence. **Journal of Early Adolescence, 6**, 29-43.

Stumphauzer, J.S. (1986). **Helping delinquents change: A treatment manual of social learning approaches.** New York: Haworth Press.

Sturge, C. (1982). Reading retardation and antisocial behavior. **Journal of Child Psychology and Psychiatry, 23**, 21-31.

Thompson, R.W., & Teare, J.F. (1997, June). **Measuring outcomes across a continuum of programs in the managed care environment.** Paper presented at the Professional Child Care Conference, Boys Town, NE.

Wadsworth, M. (1979). **Roots of delinquency: Infancy, adolescence and crime.** New York: Barnes & Noble.

Werry, J.S., & Quay, H.C. (1971). The prevalence of behavior symptoms in younger elementary school children. **American Journal of Orthopsychiatry, 41**, 136-143.

West, D.J. (1982). **Delinquency: Its roots, careers and prospects.** Cambridge, MA: Harvard University Press.

Willner, A.G., Braukmann, C.J., Kirigin, K.A., Fixsen, D.L., Phillips, E.L., Wolf, M.M. (1975, September). Training and validation: Youth preferred social behavior with child care personnel. In C.J. Braukmann (chair), **New directions in behavioral group home research.** Symposium conducted at the 83rd Annual Convention of the American Psychological Association, Chicago.

Wolfgang, M.E., Figlio, R., & Sellin, T. (1972). **Delinquency in a birth cohort.** Chicago: University of Chicago Press.

Wood, M.M., & Long, N.J. (1991). **Life space intervention.** Austin, TX: PRO-ED, Inc.

Index

Credits

Content Specialist: Tom Dowd
Editing: Terry L. Hyland
Production: Mary Steiner
Cover Design: Valerie McCormick
Page compostion: Valerie McCormick & Anne Hughes

9902-19-0003